"The world was peopled
with wonders."

The origin of Wildsam comes from above, a
line of prose in the novel *East of Eden*, written by
John Steinbeck. Six words hinting at a broad and
interwoven idea. One of curiosity, connection, joy. And
the belief that stories have the power to unearth the
mysteries of a place—for anyone. The book in
your hands is rooted in such things.

Our list of gratitude stretches throughout the borough and
beyond. First, to the editorial contributors who helped bring
the Brooklyn soul to these pages: Margaret Eby, Tim Irwin,
Sadie Stein, Brooke Porter Katz, Wesley Verhoeve, Mikki
Brammer, Sarah Gearhart, Scott Ellman and Ben Barnes. To our
first edition city editor, Gina Hamadey, our genuine appreciation
for your Brooklyn smarts and dedication. A special thank you
to the Brooklyn Historical Society and their archival staff; the
Brooklyn Public Library; Tom Hinkel and Laura Shunk at *The
Village Voice*; Nick Fauchald and Kaitlyn Goalen at Short Stack
Editions; Halimah Marcus at *Electric Literature*; and Allison
Freedman Weisberg at Recess.

WILDSAM FIELD GUIDES™

Published in the United States
by Wildsam Field Guides, Austin, Texas.

ISBN 978-1-4671-9964-3

Illustrations by Lauren Tamaki and Gabriella Trujillo

To find more field guides, please visit
www.wildsam.com

CONTENTS

*Discover the people and places
that tell the story of Brooklyn*

WELCOME

—

HERE'S A MEMORY. On an October afternoon in 2009, a loose acquaintance calls, asking for help packing up an apartment later that night. It was a fourth-floor walkup in Brooklyn Heights, and there would be beer. A common proposal in Brooklyn, where people shed apartments with the seasons. But then, less common: "Clara from Brooklyn College thought you'd be interested," the caller said. "It's Norman Mailer's place."

The sky was clear that evening. Even though he'd died two years before, the apartment looked as if Mailer had just stepped out to buy bread. Newspaper folded on the table. Coffee beans in the cupboard. Six or seven lamps glowing, books crammed everywhere, the balcony door wide open and letting in a calm breeze as the BQE hummed below. And from the windows, Mailer's evening view across the river of the giant glass city, lit up from within. What happens to you if this is where you live and this is what you see every day?

This is Brooklyn. Even for the deeper neighborhoods—Crown Heights, Bedford-Stuyvesant, Bensonhurst, Canarsie, Mill Basin— Brooklyn begins with its proximity. It wrestles with what James Agee called the "mad magnetic energy" that burns nonstop across the East River. For hundreds of years, the tension between that place and this one, of what is and what can be, has given Brooklyn the dynamism it needs to thrive. For the no-name screenwriter and the playground point guard, for the man who'd be mayor and the woman who'd sit on the Supreme Court, for the Italian restaurateur and the Haitian cab driver—for them and for millions of others across the years, Brooklyn is the proving ground. It is our most fertile urban soil for American narratives: the stranger in a strange land, the underdog, the self-made striver.

Mel Brooks and Mos Def, Barbra Streisand and Lena Horne, Sandy Koufax and Spike Lee. And the nearly four centuries of immigrant families, whose immeasurable risk and hustle and ambition formed the American mystique. Our country's soul grows from widespread roots, but in big ways, it came from these 71 square miles. It came from Brooklyn. —The Editors

ESSENTIALS

TRANSPORT

CITY APP
Transit
transitapp.com

....

FERRY
NYC Ferry
ferry.nyc

....

BIKE SHARE
Citi Bike
citibikenyc.com

LANDMARKS

GRAND ARMY PLAZA
Flatbush Ave
Olmsted-designed traffic hub and
Prospect Park sentinel.

....

BROOKLYN BRIDGE
Adams St and Tillary St
Neo-Gothic stone towers and
steel cables span the East River.

....

MEDIA

JOURNAL
The Brooklyn Rail
Local arts, culture and politics
reporting online and in print.

....

BOOKS COVERAGE
Vol. 1 Brooklyn
Smart book reviews and essays.

....

MUSIC BLOG
BrooklynVegan
News, gossip and live events.

GREEN SPACE

PROSPECT PARK
Prospect Park West
A bandshell, a zoo, an ice rink
and grassy picnic spots aplenty.
The borough's 526-acre heart.

....

MCCARREN PARK
776 Lorimer St
North Brooklyn gathering spot
for sports and carousing.

....

FORT GREENE PARK
Dekalb Avenue
Walt Whitman pushed to turn
the historic fort into a public park.

CALENDAR

JAN – APR
Coney Island Polar Bear Plunge
Lunar New Year
Cherry Blossom Festival

MAY – AUG
Five Boro Bike Tour
Celebrate Brooklyn
Hip-Hop Festival
West Indian Carnival

SEP – DEC
Atlantic Antic
BAM Next Wave Festival
Dyker Heights Lights

BOOKS
↠ *Brookyn Is* by James Agee
↠ *Another Brooklyn* by Jacque-
line Woodson
↠ *M Train* by Patti Smith

FRIDAY
Study up at City Reliquary
Steaks at Peter Luger
Maison Premiere nightcap

....

SATURDAY
Brunch at Tom's Restaurant
Brooklyn Botanic Garden wander
Beers at Threes Brewing
Dinner at Rucola

....

SUNDAY
Browse Brooklyn Flea in DUMBO
Brooklyn Bridge Park
    people-watching
Ice cream at Ample Hills

MEMENTOS

Brooklyn Cyclones cap, *Brooklyn Cyclones Official Store*, $37
Chic throw, *Dusen Dusen*, $180
Crown Heights socks, *Park Delicatessen*, $10

RECORD COLLECTION

Beastie Boys	*Licensed to Ill*
Jay-Z	*The Blueprint*
TV on the Radio	*Dear Science*
Buddy Rich	*Rich Versus Roach*
Ol' Dirty Bastard	*Return to the 36 Chambers*
Sharon Jones & the Dap-Kings	*Learned the Hard Way*
Notorious B.I.G.	*Ready to Die*
Big Daddy Kane	*Long Live the Kane*
The National	*Boxer*
MC Lyte	*Lyte as a Rock*
Sleigh Bells	*Treats*
Richie Havens	*Mixed Bag*
Vivian Girls	*Memory*
Black Star	*Mos Def & Talib Kweli Are Black Star*

ESSENTIALS

LODGING

Wythe Hotel
80 Wythe Ave
Converted factory on the Williamsburg waterfront, where concrete floors meet skyline views.

....

1 Hotel Brooklyn Bridge
60 Furman St
Sustainability made elegant. Native plants echo the Brooklyn Bridge Park setting.

....

The William Vale
111 N 12th St
Take a languid swim in the vast pool or wander the undulations of the public rooftop park.

The Box House Hotel
77 Box St
Colorful touches warm a former factory at Greenpoint's quiet northern tip.

....

The Tillary Hotel
85 Flatbush Ave Ext
With art deco flourishes and a secret cocktail bar, a homey haven amid Downtown Brooklyn bustle.

....

The Hoxton
97 Wythe Ave
Classy rooftop bar, cleverly compact rooms with Dusen Dusen linens. London vibes, NYC vistas.

COFFEE

Devoción
Williamsburg

....

Hungry Ghost
Prospect Heights

....

Loud Baby
Prospect Lefferts

....

Playground
Bed-Stuy

....

Parlor
Navy Yard

BOOKSTORES

Unnameable
Prospect Heights

....

Greenlight
Fort Green

....

Books Are Magic
Cobble Hill

....

POWERHOUSE Arena
DUMBO

....

Community
Park Slope

....

WORD
Greenpoint

WELLNESS

Urban Asanas
Warm and welcoming yoga studio. At Breath + Beats events, flow to a live DJ. *843 Sterling Pl*

....

HealHaus
Inclusive space for meditation, yoga, massage, energy healing and more. *1082 Fulton St*

....

Mermaid Spa
Eucalyptus steam, ice pools, birch venik massage. Tasty dumplings too. *3703 Mermaid Ave*

ISSUES

Housing Costs	In 2021, median home prices surged to $900,000 and rent to $2,395 a month. Evictions [despite a pandemic moratorium] continued to disproportionately affect residents of color and highlight the longstanding link between housing policies and racism in Brooklyn. **EXPERT:** *Nicole Gelinas, Manhattan Institute*
Bike Lanes	In an effort to reduce traffic, the borough aims to create 300 miles of bike lanes in the next four years with a $58.4 million bike safety plan. Work begun in 2021 includes a two-way, 8-foot-wide bike lane on the pedestrian-laden Brooklyn Bridge. **EXPERT:** *Felicia Park-Rogers, Tri-State Transportation Campaign*
Bed Bugs	The infamous NYC equalizer, these shrewd, acrobatic commuters thrive in Brooklyn's close quarters. Disease transmission isn't a risk, just sleepless nights and the creeping anxiety that they may continue to lurk. **EXPERT:** *Billy Swan, NYC Pest Control*
Police Accountability	Despite massive reductions, the legacy of former NYC Mayor Giuliani's "stop-and-frisk" and "broken windows" policies—intended to mitigate dangerous crime by policing minor offenses—lives on. In 2020, NYC recorded just 9,544 stops, a new low. But New Yorkers of color comprised 91 percent of those stops, the majority of which occurred in Brooklyn. **EXPERT:** *Mark Winston Griffith, Brooklyn Movement Center*

STATISTICS

$3,420.24	Average price of a two-bedroom in May 2021
10,000+	Protesters at June 4, 2020, George Floyd memorial
76	Hot dogs Joey Chestnut ate in 2021 Coney Island contest
68	Seasons the Dodgers played in Brooklyn
10 ft	Thickness of toxic "black mayonnaise" in Gowanus Canal
1 cent	Cost to cross Brooklyn Bridge on opening day, 1883
3,069.6	Tons of garbage collected daily

NEIGHBORHOODS

WILLIAMSBURG/GREENPOINT

Height of mid-aughts hip.

LOCAL: *Lilia, The Commodore, Chez Ma Tante*

....

BUSHWICK

Williamsburg's scrappier neighbor draws artsy 20-somethings.

Local: *Tortilleria Mexicana Los Hermanos, Bunker, Mood Ring*

....

BED-STUY/CROWN HEIGHTS

Historic Black areas with Caribbean food and brownstones.

LOCAL: *Weeksville Heritage Center, Peaches, King Tai*

....

FORT GREENE

Brownstone-lined blocks surround the namesake park.

LOCAL: *Miss Ada, BAM*

....

RED HOOK

Peninsula with shipping yards and small-town vibe.

LOCAL: *Red Hook Tavern, Sunny's Bar, Pioneer Works*

....

CARROLL GARDENS

Leafy streets, Italian roots.

Local: *Buttermilk Channel, Ugly Baby, Lucali*

PARK SLOPE

Family-oriented stretch of cozy indie shops and organic grocery stores parallels Prospect Park.

LOCAL: *al di la, Ginger's, Union Hall*

....

GOWANUS

Tattoo shops and sprawling bars have redefined a former industrial area.

Local: *Insa, Brooklyn Boulders*

....

SUNSET PARK

Diverse working-class zone with robust Chinese, South and Central American food scenes.

LOCAL: *Bamboo Garden, Tacos Matamoros, Melody Lanes*

....

BAY RIDGE

Hub for eclectic Irish, Greek, Middle Eastern and Norwegian mom-and-pop eateries.

LOCAL: *Tanoreen, The Wicked Monk, Gino's*

....

BRIGHTON BEACH

Tight-knit home to Eastern European immigrants, casual cafes, import-heavy markets.

LOCAL: *Tatiana, Brighton Bazaar*

BROOKLYN NEIGHBORHOODS ▶

GREENPOINT

WILLIAMSBURG

DUMBO

BROOKLYN HTS
FORT GREENE
COBBLE HILL
BOERUM HILL
CARROLL GARDENS
RED HOOK
GOWANUS
PARK SLOPE
PROSPECT LEFFERTS GARDENS

CLINTON HILL

BUSHWICK

BED-STUY

PROSPECT HTS

CROWN HTS

BROWNSVILLE

EAST NEW YORK

SUNSET PARK
DITMAS PARK

EAST FLATBUSH
CANARSIE

BOROUGH PARK

FLATLANDS

BAY RIDGE

DYKER HTS
MIDWOOD
BENSONHURST

BERGEN BEACH

MILL BASIN

GRAVESEND

SHEEPSHEAD BAY

MANHATTAN BEACH

CONEY ISLAND

BRIGHTON BEACH

BESTS

A curated list of city favorites—classic and new—from bars and restaurants to shops and experiences, plus a handful of can't-miss experts

FOOD & DRINK

For a map of international treats from across the borough,
see page 52.

PIZZA
Totonno's
1524 Neptune Ave
Coney Island
A strong contender in NYC's never-ending debate, this pie palace has been legit since 1924.

....

CARIBBEAN
Ali's Trinidad Roti Shop
1267 Fulton St
Crown Heights
Beloved no-frills counter spot for Trinidadian pholourie and doubles.

....

BRUNCH
Farm on Adderley
1108 Cortelyou Rd
Ditmas Park
Omelets and English-muffin burgers in a dreamy garden. Save room for the chocolate bread.

INSTITUTION
Peter Luger
178 Broadway
Williamsburg
Time-travel to old Brooklyn to hobnob with a martini and a porterhouse and spicy house sauce.

....

DINER
Tom's Restaurant
782 Washington Ave
Prospect Heights
Breakfast and lunch stalwart slinging all manner of pancakes since 1936. Try the lime rickey.

....

OYSTERS
Maison Premiere
298 Bedford Ave
Williamsburg
Line up a dozen on the half-shell at the marble U-bar and partake in the absinthe drip.

NEW AMERICAN
Olmsted
659 Vanderbilt Ave
Prospect Heights
Buzzy high Brooklyn spot with Michelin and Beard nods. Backyard garden inspires the menu.

....

SANDWICHES
David's Brisket House
533 Nostrand Ave
Bed Stuy
Classic piled-high pastrami, corned beef and brisket. Deli done right.

....

NEW-SCHOOL PIZZA
Roberta's
261 Moore Street
Bushwick
Ever-rotating menu of innovative pies, celebrity clientele. Pairs perfectly with a gallery opening.

SURF & TURF

Gage & Tollner

372 Fulton St
Downtown Brooklyn

Peak retro-chic fare:
steaks, oysters and
Baked Alaska.

....

ITALIAN

Frankies 457
Spuntino

457 Court St
Carroll Gardens

Elevated takes
on classics; killer
Sunday gravy.

....

PERSIAN

Sofreh

75 St Marks Ave
Prospect Heights

Rich saffron rice, cu-
cumber yogurt dip,
creamy desserts.

....

BREAKFAST

Marlow & Sons

81 Broadway
Williamsburg

A two-top by the
open window, one
egg-cheese biscuit
and a *Diner Journal*.

....

THAI

Ugly Baby

407 Smith St
Carroll Gardens

Well-spiced curries,
sour beer pairings.

SOUL FOOD

Mitchell's

617A Vanderbilt Ave
Prospect Heights

Your fried chicken
and cornbread fix,
right in Brooklyn.

....

BRASSERIE

Francie

134 Broadway
Williamsburg

Michelin-star fancy
fare: caviar, crown of
duck, a cheese cart!

....

BBQ

Fette Sau

354 Metropolitan Ave
Williamsburg

No plates or menus,
just trays of patiently
smoked meats.

....

SEAFOOD

Petite Crevette

144 Union St
Carroll Gardens

A cozy, fishmonger-
ish room where the
lobsters leap off the
menu.

....

DOUGHNUTS

Fan-Fan

448 Lafayette Ave
Bed-Stuy

Eclair-like fan-fans
in rotating flavors.
Sticky buns too.

COCKTAILS

Long Island Bar

110 Atlantic Ave
Cobble Hill

Same old neon
marquee, fancy new
concoctions. Best ice
in the borough.

....

BEER

Tørst

615 Manhattan Ave
Greenpoint

Minimal but cool
Danish brewers'
room, 21 taps.

....

HANGOUT

Lavender Lake

383 Carroll St
Gowanus

Grab your usual and
a spot outside under
the twinklies, repeat.

....

DIVE

Montero's Bar

73 Atlantic Avenue
Brooklyn Heights

Beloved sailors' bar.
Karaoke nights draw
devoted regulars.

....

GARDEN BAR

Sycamore

1118 Cortelyou Rd
Ditmas Park

Flower shop in the
front, epic bourbon
selection in the back.

SHOPPING

ANTIQUES

Holler & Squall
304 Henry St
Brooklyn Heights
Ever-evolving industrial and mid-century collection, guarded by a herd of taxidermy.

....

BUTCHER

The Meat Hook
397 Graham Ave
Williamsburg
Housemade cold cuts, dry-aged NY beef and thick bacon dreams—right off the BQE.

....

PLANTS

Natty Garden
636 Washington Ave
Prospect Heights
Black-owned nursery and garden supply. Stock up on city-friendly succulents and low-light ZZs.

RECORDS

Human Head
289 Meserole St
Bushwick
Mannequin heads on the ceiling, expert vinyl picks in the bins. Great genre range.

....

FOUND OBJECTS

Brooklyn Flea
Williamsburg Sat.
DUMBO Sun.
Endlessly browsable neighborhood bazaar for all things BK artisanal and antique.

....

DENIM

Brooklyn Denim Co.
338 Wythe Ave
Williamsburg
Classic and small-batch indigo, including First Standard Co.'s unique handmade jeans.

APPAREL

Front General Store
143 Front St
DUMBO
Vintage treasures and new finds with old-school trading-post vibes. Americana of the best kind.

....

WOMENSWEAR

Sincerely, Tommy
343 Tompkins Ave
Bed-Stuy
Dresses and more in stylishly bold prints, plus accessories, home goods and in-house coffee bar.

....

OUTDOORS

Hatchet Outdoor Supply Co.
77 Atlantic Ave
Brooklyn Heights
High-quality gear and garb for the adventuring urbanite. Staff knows their stuff.

JEWELRY
Catbird
219 Bedford Ave
Williamsburg
Delicate, trendsetting pieces. Basically invented the stack.

....

RUGS
Heirloom
81 Grand St
Williamsburg
Unusual handmade rugs, vintage and contemporary.

....

ART BOOKS
Spoonbill & Sugartown
218 Bedford Ave
Williamsburg
Thick stacks for the eclectic thumber.

....

GIFTS
From Here to Sunday
567 Union St
Gowanus
Small-batch goods, from bath fizzes to funfetti cookies.

....

SKATEBOARDS
Park Delicatessen
712 Classon Ave
Crown Heights
Florist plus skateboard supply. Snappy streetwear too.

THRIFT SHOP
L Train Vintage
1377 Dekalb Ave
Bushwick
Local mini-chain for an affordable wardrobe refresh.

....

HERBAL MEDICINE
Radicle
394 Atlantic Ave
Boerum Hill
Palo santo, tea and tinctures from angelica to violet.

....

SPECIALTY MARKET
Fei Long Market
6301 8th Ave
Sunset Park
Shrimp chips, woks, Sichuan peppercorns.

....

SURF
Pilgrim Surf + Supply
68 N 3rd St
Williamsburg
Longboards and wetsuits for Rockaway weekends.

....

COOKBOOKS
Archestratus
160 Huron St
Greenpoint
Munch chef Paige Lipari's arancine, then browse books and Italian groceries.

GOURMET GROCER
Foragers
56 Adams St
DUMBO
Their upstate farm supplies fresh produce and heritage eggs.

....

BICYCLES
Redbeard Bikes
69 Jay St
DUMBO
Gawk at the wall of Brompton folding bikes, then try one.

....

ARTISTS' SUPPLY
Artist & Craftsmen Supply
307 2nd St
Park Slope
One-stop shop for looms, yarns and filbert paintbrushes.

....

SPIRITS
Simple Syrup
810 Nostrand Ave
Crown Heights
Come for the curated collection of funky natural wines.

....

BEER
Beer Witch
460 Bergen St
Park Slope
Local brews to taste and take home.

ACTION

For maps exploring the arts and outdoor adventures,
see pages 64 and 68.

MOVIE THEATER

Nitehawk Cinema
136 Metropolitan Ave
Williamsburg
Enjoy film-inspired
food and cocktails
while you watch.
Overturned Prohibi-
tion-era liquor law!
....

LIVE MUSIC

Jalopy Theatre
315 Columbia St
Red Hook
Host Feral Foster's
free weekly Roots n'
Ruckus variety show
has become a folk-
music scene fixture.
....

PERFORMANCE

Brooklyn Academy
of Music
Fort Greene
Music, theater,
dance, opera, talks,
films—a cultural
touchstone for
adventurous art.

ART MUSEUM

Brooklyn Museum
200 Eastern Parkway
Prospect Heights
Beaux-arts building
holds a collection of
1.5 million works,
including a center
for feminist art.
....

COOKING

Hudson Table
88 Withers Street
Williamsburg
Hands-on classes
from Taco Night to
Japanese Surf and
Turf. Classes for
kids too.
....

DANCING

Friends and Lovers
641 Classon Ave
Crown Heights
DJs, theme nights,
plenty of soul. Let
loose at the monthly
Future Old School
hip-hop party.

PICK-UP BALL

Pier 2
150 Furman St
Brooklyn Heights
Lace 'em up tight:
these five courts
with skyline views
are BK's best spot to
run full-court.
....

PARADE

West Indian Day
Parade
Crown Heights
Join the cheers for
Caribbean paraders
in magnificently
colorful and feather-
ful costumes.
....

BOWLING

Melody Lanes
461 37th St
Sunset Park
Retro alley. Barman
Peter Napolitano
has mixed cocktails
and wisdom for
more than 30 years.

CLASSES

Brooklyn Brainery
190 Underhill Ave
Prospect Heights
Low-key lessons,
from watercolors to
whiskey history.

....

ARTS EDUCATION

MoCADA
80 Hanson Pl
Fort Greene
Trailblazing African
diaspora museum
where art meets
social justice.

....

HISTORIC HOME

Wyckoff House
5816 Clarendon Rd
East Flatbush
Built in 1652 by
Dutch immigrants,
oldest house in NYC.

....

SHUFFLEBOARD

Royal Palms
514 Union St
Gowanus
Ten rentable courts,
tropical drinks and
vibes to match.

....

SAILING

Brooklyn Sail
159 Bridge Park Dr
Brooklyn Heights
Greet Lady Liberty
and Governors Is-
land from the water.

BOXING

Gleason's Gym
130 Water St
DUMBO
Legendary spot
with five rings, $25
for a single day.

....

BLACK HISTORY

Weeksville Heritage
Center
158 Buffalo Ave
Crown Heights
Preserving one of
the U.S.'s first free
Black communities.

....

SWIMMING POOL

McCarren Park
776 Lorimer St
Williamsburg
Cool off with the
summer crowds
after a park wander.

....

CLIMBING

The Cliffs
99 Plymouth St
DUMBO
Under the Manhat-
tan Bridge, boulder-
ing with a view.

....

RUNNING ROUTE

Prospect Park Loop
Park Drive
Prospect Park
Just over 3 leafy
miles, with lanes
for bikes and peds.

CHURCH SERVICE

Brooklyn Tabernacle
Choir
17 Smith St
Downtown Brooklyn
Snag a pew for
Grammy-winning
booming gospel.

....

SUMMER SERIES

Rooftop Films
rooftopfilms.com
Indie screenings
across the borough.
Two thumbs up for
Industry City venue.

....

KARAOKE

Insa
328 Douglass St
Gowanus
Korean BBQ, private
karaoke rooms. Your
whole night, settled.

....

WATERFRONT PARK

Transmitter Park
Greenpoint Ave
Greenpoint
Lounge on the lawn;
watch the skyline
from the pier.

....

BOCCE

Union Hall
702 Union St
Park Slope
Velvet sofas and
lanes upstairs, music
venue downstairs.

EXPERTISE

RARE GUITARS
Retrofret Guitars
retrofret.com
Steven Uhrik's string-nerd haven. Pick around for a 1932 Gibson L-4 or maybe a Snakehead mandolin.

....

PIANO MOVING
Bill Rogers
thepianomover.com
Carefully hoisting baby grands up to fourth-floor walkups and barely tickling the ivories. Tuning and restoration too.

....

STREET PHOTOGRAPHY
Andre D. Wagner
@photodre
Trains his lens on everyday moments that explore questions of race, class and identity in sharp black and white.

TATTOOS
Flyrite
flyritetattoo.nyc
Williamsburg studio admired for the cleanest of lines across styles. For script, Mike Lucena is your guy.

....

FLORAL DESIGN
LaParis Phillips
@brooklynbloomsnyc
Vibrant arrangements in vintage vases, inspired by a fashion background. Shop fave: chocolate sunflowers.

....

CLIMATE SOLUTIONS
Ayana Elizabeth Johnson
ayanaelizabeth.com
Marine biologist, host of *How to Save a Planet* podcast, Urban Ocean Labs co-founder and more.

RUNNING
North Brooklyn Runners
northbrooklyn runners.org
Train to race with weekly runs starting in McCarren Park and Prospect Park.

....

FICTION WRITING
Joshua Henkin
joshuahenkin.com
Award-winning novelist directs fiction program at Brooklyn College's popular, rigorous MFA.

....

ROBOTS
Chico MacMurtrie
amorphicro botworks.org
Building robotic sculptures in a Red Hook lab housed in former Norwegian Seamen's Church.

LETTERPRESS

The Arm

thearm.org

Reserve solo time on a giant Vandercook or ink up your fingers in workshops.

....

BED BUGS

Bed Bug Inspection Group

bedbuginspection group.com

Jon and his sniffer beagle are pros; hope you won't need 'em.

....

MOTORCYCLE RESTORE

Moto Borgotaro

motoborgotaro.com

Tune-ups and custom rebuilds worth saving up for.

....

PODCASTING

Jenna Weiss-Berman

pineapple.fn

Accomplished radio producer who co-founded Pineapple Street Studios with Max Linsky.

....

CHEF

Libby Willis

@libbylark

Turned MeMe's Diner [RIP] into queer feminist pop-up cafe KIT.

CONTEMPORARY ART

Kimberly Drew

@museummammy

Curator, author and activist behind the influential Black Contemporary Art Tumblr.

....

DANCE INSTRUCTION

Cynthia King

cynthiakingdance.com

Classes from ballet to contemporary, from toddlers on up.

....

HEALTH EQUITY

Dr. Uché Blackstock

@uche_blackstock

Founded Advancing Health Equity to combat racism in health care.

....

BROWNSTONE RENO

MADE

designbuildmade.com

Designers and contractors share one roof in this non-traditional firm.

....

BLACK BUSINESSES

Aurora James

aurorajames.com

Brother Vellies founder created 15 Percent Pledge to promote Black-owned biz.

TAILOR

Fulani Boutique

fulaniboutique.com

Top-notch tapering, alterations and suiting fixes for every level of dandy.

....

LOCKSMITH

M&D Locksmith

brooklynmanhattan locksmith.com

Trustworthy, speedy and professional. Ask for Joey.

....

LIGHTING DESIGN

Workstead

workstead.com

Minimalist chandeliers and lamps, bent steel sophistication seen in Wythe Hotel.

....

DOG GROOMING

Sonia's Pet Grooming

soniaspetgrooming.com

Happy yelps from all the local pups.

....

FIBER ARTS

Caroline Kaufman

@carolinekaufman

Channeling childhood playfulness through bright patterns and tufted textures.

MORE THAN 25 ENTRIES
Excerpts have been edited for clarity and concision.

ALMANAC

*A deep dive into the cultural heritage of
Brooklyn through news clippings, lost letters, timelines,
nomenclature and other historical hearsay*

BROOKLYN DODGERS

In the late 1800s, Brooklyn dubbed its baseball club the "Trolley Dodgers," a nod to the newly electric, often dangerous trolley cars. By the 1940s, the team was simply the Dodgers, playing their home games at Ebbets Field in Flatbush and breaking the baseball color line in 1946 with Jackie Robinson. Ten years later, owner Walter O'Malley decided to uproot for sunny Los Angeles. When borough president John Cashmore heard the rumor, he sent this telegram.

SEPT 8 1957

DEAR WALTER

      REPORTS HERE INDICATE LOS ANGELES REPRESENTATIVE HAS CONFERRED WITH YOU THIS MORNING MY EARNEST SUGGESTION IS THAT YOU WITHHOLD FINAL COMMITMENT WITH THEM I AM STRIVING TO ARRIVE AT SOLUTION OF THE PROBLEM HERE AS YOU KNOW REPORT IS PENDING ON LEGALITY OF MAKING LAND AVAILABLE FOR DODGER STADIUM IT IS EXPECTED MOMENTARILY. AS I TOLD YOU I AM DOING EVERYTHING POSSIBLE TO SEE THAT THE BEST INTEREST OF THE CITY THE TAXPAYERS AND BROOKLYN DODGERS-- AND ESPECIALLY THE PROPERTY OWNERS IN THE AREA INVOLVED ARE SAFEGUARDED. OVER AND ABOVE THIS, WALTER, ALL OF US HAVE A RESPONSIBILITY TO THE MILLIONS OF DODGER FANS WHO HAVE SUPPORTED THE DODGERS AND WANT TO SEE THEM REMAIN IN BROOKLYN. MOREOVER, ALL OF US ARE AGREED THAT AS A SYMBOL TO YOUTH AND TO THE WORLD OF SPORTS, THE DODGERS AND BROOKLYN ARE AN IMMORTAL COMBINATION. BASEBALL WILL NOT BE BASEBALL WITHOUT THE DODGERS IN BROOKLYN. AND I DON,T THINK I WOULD BE ABLE TO EVER AGAIN FACE A YOUNGSTER IN BROOKLYN OR ANYWHERE, IF I DIDNT DO EVERYTHING I COULD WITHIN REASON TO KEEP THE DODGERS IN BROOKLYN. PLEASE HOLD EVERYTHING--- AND TELL THE LOS ANGELES TO GO FIND ITSELF ANOTHER BASEBALL TEAM

      SINCERELY

        JOHN CASHMORE PRESIDENT BOROUGH OF BROOKLYN

MOBSTERS OF NOTE

Life	Nickname	Infamy
1897-1944	*Lepke*	Louis Buchalter, first boss to receive death penalty
1897-1962	*Lucky*	Charles Luciano ran Commission crime network, was granted secret WWII prison deal by gov't
1899-1947	*Scarface*	Al Capone grew up in Park Slope, face slashed while working at Brooklyn nightclub
1902-1957	*The Mad Hatter*	Albert Anastasia ruthlessly led Murder Inc. and Gambinos
1905-2002	*Joe Bananas*	After Castellammarese War, Joseph Bonanno became youngest of crime family bosses
1906-1947	*Bugsy*	Famously handsome, Benjamin Siegel became mob celebrity and Vegas financier
1906-1941	*Kid Twist*	Informant Abe Reles "fell" to death from Coney Island balcony
1906-1976	*Tick-Tock*	Jewish hitman Albert Tannenbaum was a trusted soldier for Lepke Buchalter
1910-1979	*The Cigar*	Carmine Galante, shot to death in Bushwick restaurant, cigar still in mouth
1915-1985	*Big Paulie*	Butcher's son Paul Castellano inherited Gambinos until John Gotti put hit out
1930-1981	*Sonny Black*	Williamsburg local, Dominick Napolitano, let FBI agent "Donnie Brasco" infiltrate gang
1931-1996	*Jimmy the Gent*	James Burke planned JFK Airport heist, master at bribing cops for witness names

THE BROOKLYN BRIDGE

1841	German immigrant John Roebling produces wire rope in Pennsylvania
1846	Roebling completes his first suspension bridge in Pittsburgh
1855	Roebling completes a suspension bridge in Niagara Falls
1865	Roebling's son, Washington, returns from Civil War, notably manning hot-air balloon to scout enemy before Battle of Gettysburg
1867	Roebling appointed chief engineer of the Brooklyn Bridge
1869	Standing on pilings, Roebling slips, foot is crushed, then gangrene sets in. Dies of tetanus two weeks later. Last words are "The bridge will be beautiful!" Trustees appoint Washington Roebling, 32, chief engineer.
1870	Construction begins by sinking two pneumatic, 3,000-ton caissons deep into the riverbed
1871	Brooklyn caisson finally reaches bedrock, tons of concrete poured into empty chambers
1872	Men working inside second caisson suffer from the bends. Roebling crippled by the disease, bedridden in Brooklyn Heights.
1873	Boss Tweed, bridge trustee, convicted of stealing funds
1876	First steel rope strung across towers
1878	Cables finished, steel suspenders hung from cables
1883	At 1,595 feet, the Brooklyn Bridge is completed. Roebling's wife, Emily, crosses first in a carriage.
	Opens to public May 24. The next day, 250,000 people cross.
	Toll is a penny for pedestrians, five cents for a horse
	Memorial Day panic over a rumor of collapse. Twelve people are crushed to death.
1884	P.T. Barnum takes 21 elephants over bridge to prove safety
1885	Robert Odlum, a swimming instructor from Washington, D.C., dies from bridge leap

DOMINO SUGAR

"Explosion Wrecks Big Sugar Plant"
The New York Times
June 14, 1917

FIFTEEN MEN TAKEN TO HOSPITALS, ONE DEAD, FOUR DYING—MANY STILL IN RUINS.

....

PRODUCT WAS FOR ALLIES

....

HINTS OF PLOT—FIREBOATS, ALL BROOKLYN ENGINES AND A DOZEN MORE AT WORK.

Twenty men—perhaps fifty—were buried in the debris of an eleven-story building of the American Sugar Refining Company's plant in Greenpoint, Brooklyn, last night when an explosion wrecked it.

At 1 o'clock this morning fifteen injured, one of whom died and four of whom are dying, had been taken out of the burning structure, and Fire Marshal Brophy said that at least a score of the 300 men who were at work in the building had not come out. At that time fire was raging, so that it was impossible to go into the place. Men who worked there were confident 100 men had been trapped in the building. At various hospitals between sixty and seventy men were treated for burns and other injuries.

The company has large orders for sugar for our allies and the particular building in which the explosion occurred was the structure from which refined sugar was loaded for export to Europe. Fire Marshal Brophy has started an investigation of suspicious circumstances surrounding the explosion. One guess hazarded as to its cause early this morning was that an electric spark might have caused the explosion.

Chief Kenlon said at 2:30 o'clock that the fire was under control. "How many are caught in that building there is no telling until we search it," he said, "and that can't be done for some hours yet."

The building at that time was a tottering wreck. One side had fallen in and the walls left standing were staggering so that dynamiting them was considered by the firemen. The windows for blocks in every direction had been shattered by the force of the explosion.

Lieutenant Flinn at the Lee Avenue Police Station was just receiving the report of 100 Home Defense Guards when he heard the explosion. He held them, located the fire, and sent them to the scene, where they did good work holding back the crowds, in which were the wives and children of many men working in the building, as well as the relatives of 2,000 men who worked in other parts of the plant. The police got the service of 100 Naval Reserves to help handle the crowds.

The engineer at the plant said he believed the explosion had been caused through the combustion of "sugar dust" by a spark from some source. The building was used partly as a warehouse, and the loss was estimated at $1,000,000.

With searchlights from boats in the harbor playing on the fire, which endangered the ten blocks of buildings of the great sugar plant, every piece of fire apparatus in Brooklyn, half a score of companies from Manhattan, and all the fireboats were pouring streams into the burning building at 1:30 o'clock to keep the flames from spreading.

The American Sugar Refining Company's plant in Williamsburg is its largest. It stretches from South Second Street, along Kent Avenue to Grand Street. At Third Street and Kent Avenue stood an eleven-story structure for the making of granulated sugar. It was in this building that the explosion occurred. A mixer reaches from the ground floor to the fifth floor. Just before midnight there was an explosion in this mixer which demolished the fifth, sixth, seventh, eighth, ninth, tenth, and eleventh stories, and took the roof off the structure.

The 300 men at work on the night shift scurried to the fire escapes and across a bridge which led to the top floor of a seven-story structure across Kent Avenue. Most of those who got out went by this latter route. The debris from the explosion fell back upon the building, wrecking all but its walls, and a fiercely burning fire started in the highly inflammable sugar.

MOVIES

FILM	NEIGHBORHOOD	YEAR
A Tree Grows in Brooklyn	Williamsburg	1945
The French Connection	Bensonhurst	1971
Dog Day Afternoon	Gravesend	1975
Saturday Night Fever	Bay Ridge	1977
The Warriors	Coney Island	1979
Sophie's Choice	Flatbush	1982
Once Upon a Time in America	DUMBO	1984
Moonstruck	Brooklyn Heights	1987
Do the Right Thing	Bedford-Stuyvesant	1989
Goodfellas	East New York	1990
He Got Game	Coney Island	1998
Requiem for a Dream	Brighton Beach	2000
The Squid and the Whale	Park Slope	2005
Half Nelson	Gowanus	2006

NATHAN'S FAMOUS HOT DOGS

Nathan Handwerker opened Nathan's in Coney Island in 1916, charging a nickel per dog, half the price of his competitor. Throughout the 20th century, Nathan's developed a famous fan base: President Franklin D. Roosevelt served the dogs to the king and queen of England, and had some sent to Yalta for his meeting with Churchill and Stalin. Barbra Streisand had the hot dogs shipped to London for a party, and Jacqueline Kennedy served them at the White House. In recent years the stand has gained fame for its annual hot dog eating contest. [Joey Chestnut holds the world record: 76 hot dogs in 10 minutes.] Nathan's still stands on the corner of Surf and Stillwell avenues, open 365 days a year and having closed just once, due to damage from Hurricane Sandy on October 29, 2012. After seven months and millions of dollars, Nathan's reopened with a hot dog link-cutting ceremony.

THE ELEPHANTS CROSS THE BRIDGE

New York Times
May 18, 1884

England's pet, old Jumbo, his Royal Sacredness, the white elephant, and the mighty name of Barnum added a new lustre to the bridge last night. To people who looked up from the river at the big arch of electric lights it seemed as if Noah's ark were emptying itself over on Long Island. At 9:30 o'clock 21 elephants, 7 camels, and 10 dromedaries issued from the ferry at the foot of Courtland-street. "Hooray!" shouted a small boy, "there's Jumbo!" His signal spread like a financial crisis, and soon all his tribe were leading, lining, and following the procession up Broadway to the bridge. At the order of the Superintendent of Tolls no fare was collected. The bridge rules fix the fares for man, neat cattle, and horses. The question of how much an elephant or a dromedary should pay stumped the Superintendent, and until he has solved the problem Barnum will enjoy the use of his money. The white elephant, mindful of his sacred character, followed with dignity. The other elephants shuffled along, raising their trunks and snorting as every train went by. Old Jumbo brought up the rear. As he reached Brooklyn he waved his ears in acknowledgement of a prolonged chorus of delighted "ons!" from a whole house-top full of pretty girls. In the City of Churches the procession filed through a tremendous crowd to the show grounds, at Tompkins and Fulton avenues. The wagons and the rest of the animals, under the charge of R.D. Hamilton, were transferred by the Annex and Fulton ferry. A big parade will be given on Monday morning, and the first performance will be in the afternoon.

HIP-HOP

A brief timeline of the genre's origins and evolution in New York.

1974	South Bronx block parties, DJ Kool Herc, early hip-hop
1976	DJ Afrika Bambaataa battles Disco King Mario
1979	Kurtis Blow, first rapper to sign major record deal. Sugarhill Gang's "Rapper's Delight."
1980	Decade of fat laces, dookie chains, four-finger rings
1981	The Funky 4 plus One More appear on *SNL*
	Jewish teenagers Adam Yauch, Michael Diamond, John Berry and Kate Schellenbach form the Beastie Boys
1982	Fresh Kid Ice [2 Live Crew] graduates from Tilden High in Brooklyn
1984	Rick Rubin and Russell Simmons form Def Jam
1985	Nike releases the Air Jordan I to the public
	Parental Advisory label introduced by the Recording Industry Association
	Childhood friends Q-Tip and Phife Dawg form A Tribe Called Quest in Queens
1986	Run-DMC releases *Raising Hell*, produced by Russell Simmons and Rick Rubin
	The Beastie Boys release their debut album, *Licensed to Ill*
1987	DJ Scott LaRock killed outside South Bronx housing projects
1988	*Yo! MTV Raps* debuts on television
	Russell Simmons and Rick Rubin split
	KRS-One establishes the Stop the Violence movement
1989	Spike Lee's *Do the Right Thing* with Public Enemy's "Fight the Power" as theme song
	It's a Big Daddy Thing from Bed-Stuy MC Big Daddy Kane
1990	Decade of Karl Kani, Lugz, Spike's flipped bike cap
1991	The Notorious B.I.G. featured in *The Source*'s Unsigned Hype column

1992	Wu-Tang Clan forms on Staten Island
	Daymond John launches the clothing company FUBU
1994	Notorious B.I.G.'s *Ready to Die* from Bad Boy Records
	2Pac shot and robbed in New York recording studio
1995	Mobb Deep's "Shook Ones [Part II]"
1996	Bed-Stuy's Lil' Kim reaches #11 on *Billboard* chart
1997	Notorious B.I.G. is killed in drive-by shooting in Los Angeles
1998	Jay-Z releases *Vol. 2 … Hard Knock Life* on Roc-A-Fella
1999	*The Miseducation of Lauryn Hill* wins Grammy for Album of the Year
	Big L is killed in a drive-by shooting in Harlem
2000	Decade of Rocawear, throwback jerseys, grillz
2001	Puff Daddy changes name to P-Diddy
	Nas and Jay-Z public feud via Hot 97 FM face-off
2002	Jam Master Jay shot and killed in Queens, Run-D.M.C. disbands
2003	50 Cent's *Get Rich or Die Tryin'* goes platinum, will sell 15 million copies
2004	Fort Greene native Ol' Dirty Bastard collapses and dies in Manhattan
2005	Lil' Kim convicted of conspiracy, perjury over involvement in HOT 97 shooting
2006	Beyoncé, Jay-Z named *Time* magazine's most powerful couple
2011	Beginning of Jay-Z and Kanye West's *Watch the Throne* tour
2012	Run-DMC re-forms
	Blue Ivy Carter, daughter of Beyoncé and Jay-Z, born
2013	Beyoncé sings "Star-Spangled Banner" at President Obama's second inauguration
	Jay-Z starts sports agency, releases *Magna Carta Holy Grail*
2014	Twentieth anniversary of Nas' landmark album *Illmatic*
2020	Fivio Foreign and Lil Tjay make *XXL*'s Freshman Class list

GOLDEN ERA OF COMICS

A sampling of characters born from the New York comic boom of the 1930s and '40s.

SUPERHERO	POWERS
Captain Marvel	*"Shazam" grants six mythical powers*
Superman	*Flight, frozen breath, super strength, X-ray vision, super hearing*
Rockman	*Abyssmian technology and equipment, toughness and combat skills*
The Atom	*Shape- and size-shifter, a physicist and professor by day*
Plastic Man	*Comedic shape-shifter, loves a good joke and slapstick humor*
Human Top	*Reformed criminal, mutant, superhuman ability to spin in circles*
The Whizzer	*Cobra venom and mongoose blood give him superhuman speed*
Captain America	*Super-soldier serum gives ultra strength, endurance, reflexes*
Aquaman	*Underwater breathing, control over sea life, super strength*
The Human Torch	*Android, fire manipulator, fire resistance*
Wonder Woman	*Super strength, telescopic vision, stunning beauty*
Batman	*Genius mind and espionage instincts, no supernatural shortcuts*
Green Lantern	*Green flame grants mystical powers, energy manipulation*
The Flash	*Sees the world in suspended animation, super-speed*

PARK SLOPE FOOD COOP

Founded in 1973, the Park Slope Food Coop is a members-only community market where all members [15,000 and counting] work 13 shifts a year at the store and receive up to 40 percent savings on groceries. Beyond the cheaper bill, the Coop has passionate political views, pulling Chilean grapes off the shelves during Pinochet's regime and boycotting Coca-Cola products over questionable labor practices. Below, a survey of member rules.

DO COMPLETE YOUR SHOPPING BEFORE YOU GET ON THE CHECKOUT LINE.
Shopping while waiting on line is uncooperative.

DO UPLOAD YOUR CART ONTO THE NOSE/FRONT END OF THE CHECKOUT.
It is the shopper's responsibility to ensure that all items are unpacked and then added to the bill. Pack up your items after they have been scanned.

DO PAY IMMEDIATELY FOR CHECKED-OUT GROCERIES.
If you need an exception to this rule [to go to the ATM, for example] speak to the Shopping Squad Leader.

DO EAT ONLY PAID-FOR FOOD.
Don't nibble away at the Coop's financial health by eating food before you pay for it!

DON'T SHOP WHEN YOU ARE 'SUSPENDED' AND BEYOND YOUR 'GRACE PERIOD.'
When you come to the Coop and are told you are "suspended," you may be given a 10-day grace period at the entrance desk. During the grace period you should resolve your suspension.

DON'T ALLOW YOURSELF TO BE CHECKED OUT BY HOUSEHOLD MEMBERS OR FAMILY MEMBERS.
This will avoid the appearance of impropriety.

LEAVES OF GRASS

When Walt Whitman, a former editor of The Brooklyn Eagle *newspaper, self-published his first collection of poetry, critical response ranged from incredulity to mockery to awe. Below, a sampling of strong opinions.*

Life Illustrated, 1855
It is like no other book that ever was written, and therefore, the language usually employed in notices of new publications is unavailable in describing it.

....

Criterion, 1855
It is impossible to imagine how any man's fancy could have conceived such a mass of stupid filth, unless he were possessed of the soul of a sentimental donkey that had died of disappointed love.

....

The Brooklyn Daily Times, 1855
Very devilish to some, and very divine to some, will appear these new poems, the *Leaves of Grass*: an attempt, as they are, of a live, naive, masculine, tenderly affectionate, rowdyish, contemplative, sensual, moral, susceptible and imperious person, to cast into literature not only his own grit and arrogance, but his own flesh and form.

The Atlantic, 1867
It is no discredit to Walt Whitman that he wrote *Leaves of Grass*, only that he did not burn it afterwards.

....

The Literary Examiner, 1856
Suppose that Mr Tupper had been banished to the backwoods ... contracting a passion for the reading of Emerson and Carlyle? Suppose him maddened by this course of reading, and fancying himself not only an Emerson but an American Shakespeare to boot. ... In that state he would write a book exactly like Walt Whitman's *Leaves of Grass*.

....

Ezra Pound
[Whitman] is America. His crudity is an exceeding great stench, but it is America. He is the hollow place in the rock that echoes with the time. ... He is disgusting. He is an exceedingly nauseating pill, but he accomplishes his mission.

ROBERT MOSES' BRIDGE PLAN

The New York Times, March 27, 1939

The proposed Battery-to-Brooklyn bridge was attacked as hastily conceived, likely to blight real estate values at the Manhattan end, undesirable for passenger vehicles, detrimental to harbor traffic and ruinous to the skyline, in a joint statement issued yesterday by the Merchants Association, the New York Chapter of the American Institute of Architects, Real Estate Board of New York, Regional Plan Association and the West Side Chamber of Commerce.

Robert Moses, returning early from Florida to defend his project, characterized the criticisms as "the same old tripe" and said he would "take care of it all tomorrow" before the City Council Committee on State Legislation.

Commenting on the charge that the bridge was unnecessary for commercial traffic from Brooklyn and undesirable for passenger cars, Mr. Moses said those were matters for the agencies that would finance the project to worry about. He said both the RFC and a syndicate of forty banking houses were keenly interested.

"The argument is absolutely false," Mr. Moses declared. "If it were true then the bridge could not be financed."

The influential and controversial Robert Moses left his stamp on infrastructure projects across the city. His Brooklyn-Battery Bridge plan was ultimately thwarted.

CROWN HEIGHTS RIOT

On August 19, 1991, conflict erupted between the Black and Orthodox Jewish residents of Crown Heights when Yosef Lifsh, in a Lubavitcher Hasidic funeral motorcade, ran a red light, killing 7-year-old Gavin Cato and injuring his cousin Angela. Later that day, in what many saw as an act of retribution, local Black youths fatally stabbed Yankel Rosenbaum, a 29-year-old visiting Australian Hasidic scholar. For the next three days, Hasidic patrols, police and the Black community violently clashed. News coverage deepened tensions, as Jewish newspapers spoke of "black agitators" and "pogroms," Black media dismissed antisemitism, and mainstream media focused on the Black community as perpetrators and the police and white communities as victims. Criticism of the police response was a key factor in Mayor Rudy Giuliani's defeat of Mayor David Dinkins, the city's first Black mayor, in the 1993 election.

THE BIG STORM

"Brooklyn Preparing to Recover From Its Effects"

The Brooklyn Daily Eagle
March 14, 1888

Has the blizzard begun again?

That question caused considerable alarm this morning. The morning began with a fall of very light snow. Not more than one-fourth of an inch came down, before the skies cleared and the sun came out and people looked down from their second story windows and thanked their stars that the storm was over.

They rejoiced too soon.

Very shortly after 11 o'clock the snow was coming down hard again and the sky was dark gray and threatening. The air was still and the clouds above looked full of snow.

"Say, boys!" said one jocular gentleman who stood on the steps of the City Hall with a group of officials who were taking a half holiday; "if the snow does not let up the banks will rise so high that the clouds will not be able to get past."

Another steady downfall of snow is no joke. Here is what it means:

That the trains of the Long Island Railroad, laden with passengers and supplies, will be buried deeper than ever in the drifts between stations.

That the trains stuck in the drifts outside New York will share the same fate.

That Brooklyn and New York will be cut off from fresh meat, milk, butter, eggs, poultry, ducks, geese and turkeys, and fresh vegetables of all kinds.

That two or three more days of impassable drifts will find the grocery stores of the city depleted, the slaughter houses empty and half the homes of the city without food or fuel.

The supplies of these cities are never more than a week ahead of their necessities and a continuation of the storm means famine for many homes.

The disasters caused by the blizzard so far have not by any means all been chronicled. Returns from the police precincts are very meager, for communications inside the city are almost entirely interrupted. The EAGLE has already reported four cases of death from the storm, ten cases of missing people and forty cases of persons overpowered by the storm, but afterward resuscitated. The number of frostbitten amounts to many hundreds. In addition to these there must be many missing in Brooklyn and its suburbs who have not yet been reported to police by reason that the relatives are snow bound in their houses.

THE EGG CREAM

There's no more nostalgic drink for Brooklynites [especially those over 50] than the egg cream—which famously includes neither egg nor cream. It started in 1904, when Herman Fox combined milk, seltzer and his own chocolate syrup. H. Fox & Co. bottled "U-bet" syrup in 1948, and introduced egg creams to a wider audience at the 1964 World's Fair in Queens. Local diners and ice cream parlors still pour the drink. Try Junior's downtown or Tom's Restaurant in Prospect Heights or Brooklyn Farmacy in Carroll Gardens—or try to make it from scratch.

....

THE ORIGINAL EGG CREAM

(1) Pour one inch of U-bet chocolate syrup into a tall, chilled, straight-sided, 8-oz. glass.

(2) Add one inch of whole milk.

(3) Tilt the glass and spray seltzer from a pressurized cylinder off a spoon to make a robust head.

(4) Stir and drink with a straw.

JACKIE ROBINSON

The Brooklyn Daily Eagle
August 24, 1949

"I'll never forget the day when a few loudmouthed guys on the other team began to take off on Peewee Reese. They were joshing him viciously because he was playing *with me* and was on the field nearby. Mind you, they were not yelling at me; I suppose they did not have the nerve to do that, but they were calling him some very vile names and every one bounced off Peewee and hit me like a machine-gun bullet. Peewee kind of sensed the sort of hopeless, dead feeling in me and came over and stood beside me for a while. He didn't say a word but he looked over at the chaps who were yelling at me through him and just stared. He was standing by me, I could tell you that. Slowly, the jibes died down like when you kill a snake an inch at a time, and then there was nothing but quiet from them. It was wonderful the way this little guy did it. I will never forget it. All the fellows on the Dodger team have worked with me in the same spirit."

SUPERNATURAL

Mollie Fancher suffered a terrible fall from a horse-drawn trolley car in 1865, after which she lost her senses of sight and touch, went weeks without eating, and confined herself to bed in Fort Greene. When Mollie later claimed to have supernatural powers, newspapers called her the "Brooklyn Enigma." Several of those mysterious claims are listed below.

- ⮡ Read unopened letters.
- ⮡ Describe articles hidden in pockets.
- ⮡ Tell time from her small gold watch, hanging across the room.
- ⮡ Read books hidden under her sheets.
- ⮡ Speak with the dead.
- ⮡ Observe her friends in the outside world, recounting details from their days.

CHESS

> "HIGH SCHOOL
> STUDENT, BOBBY
> FISCHER WINS
> U.S. CHESS
> CHAMPIONSHIP"

New York *Daily News*
January 9, 1958

Brooklyn has itself a new triple crown winner today. What Duke Snider and Roy Campanella are to baseball, 14-year-old Bobby Fischer is to the world of chess. Chess fans about the country are calling Bobby "player of the century" and "greatest chess prodigy of the age."

At a tournament completed early yesterday, at the Manhattan Chess Club, the smooth-cheeked sophomore from Erasmus Hall HS won the United States Chess Championship with a score topping 13 of the very best players in the country. With the junior championship won last July in San Francisco and the open championship garnered in August in Cleveland, Bobby today is undisputed king of the ancient sport, and probably the only player to have held all three titles at one time.

Although Bobby was not announced winner until well after midnight and he did not get back to his home at 560 Lincoln Place until 2 A.M., he attended school as usual yesterday, apparently unruffled by his unparalleled achievement. Bobby's next step is the world championship to be held in Yugoslavia next September. Bobby and another member of the American team will make the trip if sufficient funds can be raised to cover their expenses.

Bobby was to have played in Russia last summer but financial support for the tour was pledged too late. The boy turned down a bid to compete against a group of the world's chess masters at the Christmas tournament at Hastings, England, in favor of the Manhattan tourney. …

The strain of the Lessing J. Rosenwald Trophy tournament, as the masters championship is called, has been severe, according to Mrs. Fischer, and Bobby was anxious to forget chess and concentrate on his studies and on other interests—tennis, swimming, skiing and the like.

But chances are the lustre added by his latest win will bring in another spate of invitations for further exhibitions. Talk of a trip to Russia has begun again and the State Department is said to be trying to raise the money.

SPECIAL NOTICE, WANTS AND MISCELLANY

The Brooklyn Daily Eagle
July 26, 1855

BONE DUST.—FOR SALE, a pure article of bone, of a variety of fineness, from half inch to perfect powder, a great article for Grape vines or farming purposes. Apply to J.S. Mackey, 6 Court street, Brooklyn

LET THERE BE LIGHT, AND THERE was Light—now if you wish to get pure Burning Fluid. Camphene and Alcohol; also the best sperm, solar, lard and whale oil, call at Chappel & Co, 63 Fulton st. Wholesale and Retail Dealers. N. B.—Girandoles and Lamps repaired, altered and regilded.

TO NERVOUS SUFFERERS.—Rev. John M. Dagnall's celebrated IGNATIA PILLS, for the effectual cure of Nervous Weakness and Nervous Complaints of every kind, prepared by his own dispenser from his invaluable prescription, may now be obtained of all respectable druggists. Agents for Brooklyn—MRS. Hayes, 175 Fulton-st. ; T. MARSEL-US, 192 Court-st. ; D. OWEN, 154 Atlantic-st.

TO THE LADIES.
As the month of May is the time for changing houses, and the woods and flowery vallies are filled with the little songsters, so is DODGE & CO.'S STORE. Nos. 812 and 314 Fulton street, with the latest styles of FANCY BIRD CAGES, which they offer at lower prices than any other store in Brooklyn. Please call and select for yourselves.

TEETH ! TEETH !! TEETH !!!—N.B. GRIFFIN, Dental Surgeon, 276 Fulton-st. Brooklyn, would make known to the public, that he is enabled to furnish artificial teeth of superior quality of every size and color.

- ☞ *Gold Atmospheric Plates for*.....$60.00
- ☞ *Partial setts per tooth from*.....3.00 to 4.00
- ☞ *Cavities filled with Gold from*.....0.50 to 1.00
- ☞ *Full upper and under setts on Silver*.....20.00
- ☞ *Filling with Tin Foil or Cement*.....0.50
- ☞ *Extracting*.....0.25

THE NEW YORK GARBAGEMAN

E.B. White

There is no one in all New York that we envy more than the garbageman. Not even a fireman gets so much fun out of life. The jolly, jolly garbageman goes banging down the street without a thought for anyone. He clatters his cans as he listeth; he scatters ashes on the winds with never a thought that the wind-blown ash problem was settled in 1889 when the little old one-horse dump carts had covers put on them. He is shrewd in measuring his pace, and goes down the block bit by bit, innocently keeping just to windward of you. He drives like a ward boss through red lights and green, and backs his truck over the crossing with more privilege than a baby carriage on Fifth Avenue. He is as masterful as a pirate and chock-full of gusto. As we watch a garbage crew at work, we momentarily expect to see them burst into song and clink property beakers. Why shouldn't they? They have the town by the tail and they know it.

Published by
The New Yorker *on*
December 6, 1930

CLASSES

The diverse world of how-to in Brooklyn.

Six-Day Shoemaking Intensive...*Williamsburg*
Wet-Plate Photography ....*Red Hook*
Origami Folding...*Park Slope*
One-Day Neon Workshop ....*Gowanus*
Houseplant Propagation Techniques...........................*Prospect Heights*
Beginning Old-Time Fiddle...*Carroll Gardens*
Preparing Your Pet for a Baby ....*Park Slope*
Kitchen Knife Sharpening..*Bushwick*
Novice Surfing...*Rockaways*
Hula-Hoop Meditation...*Park Slope*

SANDHOGS

When the Brooklyn Bridge was built, Surgeon of the Bridge Company, Dr. Andrew Smith, made nine rules to protect diggers—called "sandhogs"—from debilitating physical effects of compromised air.

SMITH'S NINE RULES

① Never enter the caisson with an empty stomach.

② Use as far as possible a meat diet, and take warm coffee freely.

③ Always put on extra clothing on coming out, and avoid exposure to cold.

④ Exercise as little as may be during the first hour coming out, and lie down if possible.

⑤ Use intoxicating liquors sparingly; better not at all.

⑥ Take at least eight hours' sleep every night.

⑦ See that the bowels are open every day.

⑧ Never enter the caisson if at all sick.

⑨ Report at once at the office all cases of illness, even if they occur after going home.

STREET GANGS

Notorious Brooklyn affiliations in the 1970s.

- Tomahawks
- Young Barons
- Pure Hell
- Warlords
- Vanguards
- Savage Nomads
- Phantom Lords
- Dirty Ones
- Young Survivors
- Black Stabbers
- Trouble Bros.
- Outlaws
- Excons
- Latin Tops
- Wicked Ones
- Black Attacks
- Black Bulls
- Unknown Riders
- Sinners
- Mad Caps
- Spanish Kings

SHEEPSHEAD BAY

Brooklyn's quaint fishing village was once home to 50-plus "party boats," vessels that allowed anyone to hop aboard with rod and reel. As pollution increased, interest waned, and most of the fishing operations folded. However, one of the oldest Sheepshead Bay families still operates their Dorothy B. *fleet, established circa 1918.*

DOROTHY B. #1

In 1918, William Bradshaw bought a small boat—sea air was said to be good for the lead paint in his lungs—named it *Dorothy B.* after his first daughter, and docked it along Emmons Avenue.

....

DOROTHY B. #2 AND #3

In the late '20s the Bradshaws grew their fleet, each vessel bigger than the previous. They charged 50 cents for a ride, and according to William's son Walter, "For fifty cents you'd catch a sack full of fish that was enough to feed your family for a week."

....

DOROTHY B. #4

Business was good enough in 1931 that the family purchased a 45-footer, taking fishermen out onto the Atlantic Ocean for runs of fluke, mackerel, blues, cod, porgy, striped bass and blackfish.

DOROTHY B. #5

By 1950, William's sons—Joe, Frank and Walter—were running the fishing business full-time, and bought a stately boat that fit more than two dozen people.

....

DOROTHY B. #6

A sleek, 83-foot converted World War II subchaser became the pride of their fleet. In 1974, Joe, Frank and Walter retired and sold to Walter's son, Kevin.

....

DOROTHY B. #7

In 1980, Captain Kevin bought the seventh *Dorothy B.* and broke with tradition by including *"VII"* in the name.

....

DOROTHY B #8

The family's first aluminum boat is also the fastest and biggest, at 90 feet long. In 2009, Captain Kevin decided to move his business to Atlantic Highlands, New Jersey.

PARK SLOPE PLANE CRASH

December 16, 1960, began as an ordinary day in Park Slope. The corner of 7th Avenue and Sterling Place was as picturesque as ever. All that changed shortly before 11 a.m., when United Airlines Flight 826 collided midair with Trans World Airlines Flight 266, crashing into the neighborhood. Six bystanders on the ground were killed, as were all 128 passengers. The fire commissioner called it "an act of God" that the major impact of the crash had been on a vacant church rather than on surrounding buildings. One high school teacher told the *New York Herald Tribune* that he could see the pilots' faces from his classroom window just before the plane crashed. One passenger, a young boy named Stephen Baltz, was thrown from the plane and landed in a snowbank. He survived for only one day, but recounted to his rescuers on 7th Avenue that just before the plane went down, he noticed the snow falling on Brooklyn. "It looked like a picture out of a fairy book," he said.

CRIME

Selected statistics from an 1870 annual police report for the city of Brooklyn

OFFENSES AND TOTAL ARRESTS FOR THE YEAR

Bastardy	47
Bigamy	8
Cruelty To Animals	138
Disobeying Parents	1
Highway Robbery	40
Insulting Females	9
Keeping Disorderly Houses	20
Lounging	507
Malicious Mischief	433
Seduction	21
Sneak Thieving	19
Vagrancy	1,463

OCCUPATIONS OF THOSE ARRESTED

Boot-Blacks	26
Cigar-Makers	127
Errand Boys	30
Ferry Master	1
House-Keepers	2,347
Icemen	10
Japanners	7
Morocco-Dressers	29
Organ Grinders	2
Oyster Dealers	6
Rag Pickers	21
Servants	1,251

HENRY WARD BEECHER

Throughout his years at Plymouth Church in Brooklyn Heights, abolitionist preacher Henry Ward Beecher gave rousing speeches championing women's suffrage and the theory of evolution, even using the pulpit to purchase the freedom of a nine-year-old enslaved girl, Sally Marie Diggs. Controversy was Beecher's truest companion. As his lectures were published and sold throughout the country, Beecher became well known, but his fame peaked in 1875 when he stood trial for having an affair with a former colleague's wife.

In his own words:

ON SCIENCE

"The future is not in danger from the revelations of science. Science is truth; Truth loves the truth."

....

ON EQUALITY

"If any man says to me, 'Why will you agitate the woman's question, when it is the hour for the black man?' I answer, it is the hour for every man, black or white."

....

ON VOTING RIGHTS

"The truth that I have to urge is not that women have the right of suffrage—not that Chinamen or Irishmen … not that native born Yankees have the right of suffrage—but that suffrage is the inherent right of mankind."

....

ON EVOLUTION

"In respect to the fantastic notions that we sprang from monkeys … It is not where a man starts, it is where he ends."

....

ON CHRISTIANITY

"If the American people are ever driven away from the Church, and from faith in the Christian religion, it will be the fault of the Church and of the Pulpit."

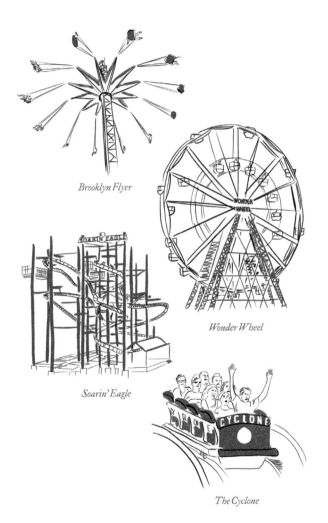

Brooklyn Flyer

Wonder Wheel

Soarin' Eagle

The Cyclone

CONEY ISLAND AMUSEMENTS OF NOTE

THE CYCLONE The Nickel Empire icon trades on more than nostalgia: the fear is the fun. Sit in back to indulge the 85-foot drops and 60 mile per hour whip turns.

....

THE THUNDERBOLT Speedy steel roller coaster replaced the wooden original. A modern marvel with throwback thrills.

....

SLINGSHOT Luna Park's gravity-defier launches riders 150 feet over Brooklyn at 90 miles per hour in an open-air cockpit.

....

WONDER WHEEL The long-promised wedding present from Constantinos Dionysios Vourderis—a.k.a. Deno—to his wife, Lula. 400,000 pounds, rising 150 feet with views for miles.

....

SPOOK-A-RAMA Ghouls, demons, damsels in distress and Frankenstein. Once billed as the longest, largest dark ride on Coney Island.

....

SOARIN' EAGLE Lie prone and ascend like America's favorite bird of prey through hairpin turns, barrel rolls and intense drops on 1,293 feet of track.

....

BROOKLYN FLYER Double-seat, open-air chairs 100 feet above the ground. On the other side of the thrill, pure wonder.

....

CONEY ISLAND RACEWAY Strap in and exercise your lead foot in gas-powered, highly maneuverable go-karts, right by the beach.

....

TORNADO ROLLER COASTER Tornado, formerly Bob's, had a hybrid design of wood track and steel structure. Destroyed by arson in 1977, demolished in '78.

....

SWITCHBACK RAILWAY Designed by LaMarcus Adna Thompson in 1881 and constructed in 1884, the first Coney Island coaster: 5 cents to go 600 feet—at 6 miles per hour.

....

FLIP FLAP RAILWAY The first looping coaster in the U.S. exerted extreme g-force on riders. Tested with sandbags and monkeys before human trials began.

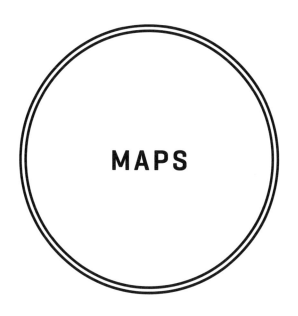

MAPS

Hand-illustrated maps to tell stories about the borough's
international cuisine, hip-hop heritage, literary life, where art
thrives, where kids play and where to find peace and quiet

Peter Pan Donut + Pastry Shop

Arepa Lady

Arepa Lady at Dekalb Market

BaXuyên

Love, Nelly

Trinidad Golden Place

БАРЕНИЧНАЯ
TEL. 718-332-9797
VARENICHNAYA

Safir Bakery + Cafe

Varenichnaya

TASTING MENU

With Brooklyn's range of international cuisine, you can hop off the subway at any stop and sample something storied and delicious.

PETER PAN DONUT & PASTRY SHOP

A North Brooklyn institution, this old-school Polish doughnut shop opens at 4:30 a.m. Come early for the full array: apple crumb, blueberry buttermilk, toasted coconut, Bavarian cream. *727 Manhattan Ave*

TRINIDAD GOLDEN PLACE

Takeout-only spot for Trinidadian-Chinese baked goods. The vegetarian roti is a beautifully spiced combination of pumpkin, chana and spinach over Trinidadian fried flatbread. *788 Nostrand Ave*

AREPA LADY

The Brooklyn anchor of Maria Piedad Cano's former food cart sells unfussy, delicious Colombian arepas de queso: sweet corn exterior, gooey cheese interior. *Dekalb Market Hall, 445 Gold St*

BA XUYÊN

An unassuming Sunset Park storefront has some of the best bánh mì in the city. Go classic: pork roll, pâté, butter, pickled veggies, head cheese and ham, all layered on crisp French bread. *4222 8th Ave*

VARENICHNAYA

Hole-in-the-wall near the boardwalk specializing in pelmeni, little Russian dumplings. The tart cherry pelmeni, served with extra cherry juice for dipping, are the star. *3086 Brighton 2nd St*

SAFIR BAKERY

This Turkish bakery and cafe may have Brooklyn's best baklava; both the pistachio and walnut versions are exceptional. Pick up a box of sweets on the way to the beach. *2724 Avenue U*

LOVE, NELLY

Airy counter-service spot serves up excellent empanadas with fillings that rotate depending on the season. Solid cup of coffee, too. *53 Rockaway Ave*

FOOD RADIO *Broadcasting 40 shows a week from two recycled shipping containers in the backyard at Roberta's, Heritage Radio Network explores food trends, chefs' stories, culinary history and more.*

LITERATURE

*Ever since Walt Whitman walked the streets, Brooklyn
has been a writer's [and reader's] haven.*

FRANKLIN PARK READING SERIES

This Crown Heights garage turned bar becomes a literary salon on the second Monday of each month. Past participants include Mary Gaitskill, Jennifer Egan and Colson Whitehead. *618 St John's Pl, franklinparkbrooklyn.com*

BROOKLYN PUBLIC LIBRARY

The columned central branch of the Brooklyn Public Library looks majestic at its perch in Grand Army Plaza. Inside are author talks and panels in addition to sci-fi film screenings and chamber music concerts. *10 Grand Army Plaza, bklynlibrary.org*

826NYC & THE BROOKLYN SUPERHERO SUPPLY CO.

At this nonprofit clubhouse, tutors teach kids and teens how to write. Also a go-to catchall for aspiring caped crusaders. *372 Fifth Ave, 826nyc.org*

BOOKS ARE MAGIC

When Cobble Hill's BookCourt shuttered in 2016, novelist Emma Straub saved local book lovers with this favorite. *225 Smith St, booksaremagic.net*

GREENLIGHT

Fort Greene's beloved bookstore has launched many local partnerships, from a kiosk at BAM to an African American reading series at Bedford Stuyvesant Restoration. *686 Fulton St, greenlightbookstore.com*

BROOKLYN INN

When Jonathan Ames' HBO show *Bored to Death* was canceled, he threw a going-away party at this century-old hangout. *148 Hoyt St*

BROOKLYN BOOK FESTIVAL

Every September, literary stars and book nerds descend on downtown Brooklyn. *brooklynbookfestival.org*

READING MATERIAL *Several innovative literary publications call Brooklyn home, including* N+1, Electric Literature, A Public Space, BOMB *and* One Story.

Norman Mailer

Books are Magic

Brooklyn Inn

826 Brooklyn Superhero Supply

Walt Whitman

Greenlight Bookstore

A Tree Grows in Brooklyn

Brooklyn Public Library

Franklin Park Reading Series

R.I.P.
MCA

Westinghouse High

Albee Square Mall

Adam Yauch Park

BIZ MARKIE

Countryhouse Diner

Brooklyn Hip Hop Festival

Marcy Projects

Chapelle's Block Party

Do The Right Thing

HIP-HOP

*From Biggie to the Beastie Boys to Spike Lee joints,
Brooklyn's influence on hip-hop culture runs deep.*

ADAM YAUCH PARK

Tucked under the BQE, this Brooklyn Heights playground was renamed in memory of the Beastie Boy who grew up around the corner.

MARCY HOUSES

The Bed-Stuy public housing complex serves as the setting for many a Jay-Z song about childhood and early forays into both hustling and rap.

COUNTRY HOUSE DINER

"A T-bone steak, cheese eggs, and Welch's grape," from Notorious B.I.G.'s song "Big Poppa," was a shout-out to this diner, down the street from 226 St. James Place, his childhood home in Clinton Hill.

WESTINGHOUSE HIGH SCHOOL

Downtown vocational school better known for lunchroom battles of freestylin' students like DMX, Busta Rhymes and others.

ALBEE SQUARE MALL

"My house is the Albee Square Mall," sings T.J. Swan on the classic Biz Markie track, written by Big Daddy Kane and named after this long-gone Brooklyn mall.

BROKEN ANGEL HOUSE

Featured as the backdrop for *Dave Chappelle's Block Party* film, featuring performances by Brooklyn's Mos Def, Talib Kweli, Dead Prez, and the reunited Fugees.

DO THE RIGHT THING

Spike Lee's epic Brooklyn joint, shot mostly in Bed-Stuy, gave a 19-year-old dancer and choreographer named Rosie Perez her first movie role.

BROOKLYN HIP-HOP FESTIVAL

Established in 2005, the BHF is NYC's largest cultural event with hip-hop at the core. Performances, panel discussions, exhibits and more.

> IN PHOTOS *In* Hip Hop at the End of the World, *Ernest Paniccioli [a.k.a. Brother Ernie] captures 40 years of hip-hop history, from the 1970s on, via 250 striking photos of rappers of note.*

KIDS

From stroller-slammed Park Slope to Coney Island's Cyclone, this borough is chockablock with children—and ways to keep them entertained.

PROSPECT PARK

At the Zucker Natural Exploration Area playground, kids play on hollowed-out stumps and balance-beam logs created from some of the 500 trees felled by Hurricane Sandy. *31 East Dr, prospectpark.org*

BROOKLYN BOTANIC GARDEN

The botanic garden is the perfect picnic destination—kids run through cherry blossoms in the spring and dry leaves in the fall. The immersive Discovery Garden gives kids of all ages a hands-on experience. *150 Eastern Parkway, bbg.org*

JANE'S CAROUSEL

French architect Jean Nouvel enclosed a 1922 carousel in an ultramodern glass shed, which now sits on the East River as part of the fantasyland [giant soccer fields, beaches, playgrounds] that is Brooklyn Bridge Park. *janescarousel.com*

NEW YORK TRANSIT MUSEUM

At this underground 1936 subway station, children board vintage subway and elevated cars. *Boerum Pl and Schermerhorn St*

BROOKLYN FARMACY & SODA FOUNTAIN

Opened in 2010, Cobble Hill has embraced this throwback, especially the maple egg creams. Stop by on Friday nights for live kids' music. *513 Henry St*

CONEY ISLAND

Hot dogs, roller coasters, the boardwalk, a mermaid parade, an aquarium and a fun minor league baseball team—Coney Island is a summer paradise.

VAN LEEUWEN

Flavors such as Sicilian Pistachio, Honeycomb and Peanut Butter Marshmallow—plus an A+ vegan list—have turned this Greenpoint-based creamery into a mini-empire in NYC. *620 Manhattan Ave, vanleeuwenicecream.com*

LOCAL EXPERT *Marcos Stafne, PhD, is the mind behind visitor experience at the fantastic Brooklyn Children's Museum, built in 1899 and the first of its kind. 145 Brooklyn Ave, brooklynkids.org*

Jane's Carousel

New York Transit Museum

Brooklyn Farmacy

Coney Island!

Luna Park

Van Leeuwen

Brooklyn Children's Musuem

Brooklyn Botanic Gardens

D.A.I.R

Pioneer Works

The Center for Urban Pedagogy

What Is Affordable Housing?

Eyebeam

Recess

Satellite Art Club

The Laundromat Project

ART AND INNOVATION

The places that keep the Brooklyn art world not just turning, but evolving.

PIONEER WORKS

Building community and promoting experimentation across the arts and sciences in a cavernous converted Red Hook factory through concerts, exhibitions, classes, artist residencies and more. *159 Pioneer St*

RECESS

Organization partners with artists to make the creative world more equitable. Session program allows artists to transform Recess, using it as both studio and immersive exhibition space. *46 Washington Ave*

EYEBEAM

Nonprofit center where diverse artists and inventors can explore the intersection of art and technology in efforts to make the future more just. *185 Wythe Ave*

THE LAUNDROMAT PROJECT

Bed Stuy-based nonprofit investing in communities of color through socially engaged art projects—originally in local laundromats, now anywhere that people gather. *1476 Fulton St*

THE CENTER FOR URBAN PEDAGOGY

Projects use art and design to tackle issues like LGBTQ rights, food access, the gender wage gap and more. *232 3rd St*

A.I.R.

Exhibition space centering women and nonbinary artists. Hosts lectures and other events about feminism and art. Founded by 20 women artists in 1972. *155 Plymouth St*

SATELLITE ART CLUB

Small but vibey dive bar and exhibition and performance space. Created in an effort to help rebuild the art scene amid the COVID-19 pandemic; $25 buys you a membership. *961 Fulton St*

STUDENT WORK *To see what the next generation of artists is cooking up, check out Pratt Institute's annual thesis exhibitions— photography, jewelry, printmaking, sculpture, performance and more—or browse portfolios online. prattshows.pratt.edu*

ESCAPES

*Finding peace and quiet in New York's
most populous borough.*

PROSPECT PARK

Designed by Frederick Law
Olmsted and Calvert Vaux of
Central Park fame. A magnet
for joggers, hikers, birders
and anyone looking to forget
they live in a concrete jungle.
prospectpark.org

....

BROOKLYN HEIGHTS PROMENADE

This ⅓-mile-long walkway
overlooking the East River and
lower Manhattan offers what
may be the best view in all of
NYC. Recipe for a respite: pack
a book, grab a bench and turn
off your phone. *Joralemon St
and Grace Ct*

....

LOUIS VALENTINO JR. PARK

Though simple, this charming
park in Red Hook gets you as
close to the Statue of Liberty
as possible in Brooklyn. There's
a pier that juts out over the
water—an ideal perch for
breezy sunset views. *Coffey St
and Ferris St*

NORTH BROOKLYN BOAT CLUB

Tucked into an alley in a not-so-
scenic part of Greenpoint, this
boathouse gives paddlers access
to hidden beaches or crowdless
water-roaming in Newtown
Creek. *51 Ash Street,
northbrooklynboatclub.org*

....

GREEN-WOOD CEMETERY

Stunning Gothic arches lead
to the resting place of notable
New Yorkers—F.A.O. Schwarz,
Boss Tweed and Jean-Michel
Basquiat among them. [Not
to mention the colonies of
blue-green monk parrots.] It's
wonderfully tranquil—hills and
valleys, glacial ponds and war
monuments. *500 25th Street,
green-wood.com*

....

MANHATTAN BEACH PARK

This quiet crescent is on the
same peninsula as crowd-heavy
Coney Island—but it's much the
opposite in vibe. *Oriental Blvd
between Ocean and Mackenzie*

DAY TRIP *For a hike beyond the city's bounds, Breakneck Ridge in the
Hudson Valley is not only jaw-droppingly gorgeous, but also accessible
by train from Grand Central on weekends and holidays.*

Brooklyn
Heights
Promenade

Louis
Valentino
Jr. Park

Take the **B**
to Brighton Beach

Manhattan
Beach
Park

Green-Wood
Cemetery

North
Brooklyn
Boat Club

Prospect Park

INTERVIEWS

———

Fourteen conversations about minor league baseball, violin-making, Spike Lee, karaoke, pizza dough, literary magazines and more

CHRISTINE SAHADI WHELAN

SHOP CO-OWNER

WHEN YOU THINK of Sahadi's, it's Charlie Sahadi—my father.

MY DAD WAS traditional. He ran the business the way he always ran it. My uncle used to count the inventory and keep it in his brain.

WHEN I FIRST started here almost 40 years ago, we had a cash register that we put in the numbers, hit plus and the next one came up.

IT TOOK YEARS to get my father to take credit cards.

MIDDLE EASTERNERS COOK. I grew up cooking with my mom, with my grandmother.

IT WAS SOMETHING that you picked up almost through osmosis: You were in the kitchen because that was, and still is, the hub of our family life.

I LOVE THAT Middle Eastern food has become so mainstream.

WHEN WE WERE growing up, hummus was not a thing. People would come in and you would have to explain what's tahini.

IT'S INTERESTING TO see the customers who eat our hummus for the first time, because we hand-make everything in our deli.

WE MAKE HUMMUS from fresh chickpeas every single day—about 2,000 pounds a week—and every one of those chickpeas is boiled in-shop.

PEOPLE READ ABOUT our hummus, and they come and buy it because if you come to Sahadi's, you buy hummus. Then they write me a note saying it was life-changing.

ONE OF MY favorite things is our roasted almonds. We roast them right here in Brooklyn. They're crisp through and through.

PEOPLE COME INTO the store for community. It's a big part of who we are.

YOU'RE OUR NEIGHBOR, you're our friends, you're a part of our community.

KEITH RAAD

BROOKLYN CYCLONES ANNOUNCER

REPS IS THE name of the game.

THE AMOUNT OF times you can get on air will make you better.

THAT'S THE REASON that a lot of guys and girls coming out of school get into minor league baseball: baseball is every single day.

IT'S AN OPEN-BOOK test every night.

WE HAVE OUR score book with the lineups for the day, stats. Every day we create game notes, with starting pitcher information and the main storylines of the team.

PEOPLE THINK I roll up to the stadium at 6:00, put the headset on, and off we go. But it's not that at all.

YOU'RE LIVING IN it. I'm amongst the players, constantly talking to them, gathering stories.

THERE'S PLAYERS THAT are tough and rigid, or diva players who have a lot of money, but everybody's weird. Everybody's got a story.

PEOPLE OF ALL shapes and sizes like to be heard.

EVERY STEP THAT I take through that stadium, I pick up something that I'm going to say that night on the air.

EVERYBODY IN THE minor leagues is putting in hours and hours and hours of work, hoping to one day get noticed and maybe call a big league game.

MY FAVORITE PLACE is the rooftop. You have the bird's eye view of the stadium, fans, the beach, the Parachute Jump, the coasters going in Luna Park and the Ferris wheel.

TURN AROUND, you see Surf Avenue and people walking to the stadium. And out in the distance, you can actually see the skyline of Manhattan.

CONEY ISLAND IS a weird place, but it's also chaotically beautiful.

SAM ZYGMUNTOWICZ

LUTHIER

EVERY VIOLIN I make is destined for someone.

START TO FINISH, one takes about six months.

I READ A BOOK about a violin-maker when I was 13 and just got captivated.

I CAME TO Brooklyn in 1980 right out of violin-making school. My brother lived in Park Slope, and I slept on his floor.

WHEN YOU'RE making an instrument, you're making it for a specific purpose, and you can judge whether it's good or not. It's not subject to whim like the world of fine art.

I DON'T TALK about cost.

I'M ALWAYS sourcing wood. It's kind of like having a wine cellar.

TOPS ARE MADE of spruce. Of the European woods, it's the lightest per unit of weight. Makes it very resonant. Backs and sides and necks are maple.

I LEARNED FROM a French teacher there's proper use of the knife, a lot of body mechanics in it. You learn how to control force, apply it with great control and delicacy.

YOU CAN'T BELIEVE that something this light can fill an entire concert hall with sound.

YOU HAVE TO feel the authority of your teacher. Not because they're your boss, but because they're a master.

I WAS ASKED by Isaac Stern to copy his Guarneri. At the time, Stern was the king. It was very intimidating to simultaneously work for one of the great musicians of all time and reproduce one of the greatest violins in history.

BUT WE LIVE in the same physical universe, we use the same materials. If it was doable by them, it's doable by me.

THERE'S NOTHING so good that it can't be better.

ROSIE PEREZ

ACTRESS

I LIVED IN North Bushwick with my aunt. She worked two factory jobs, one as a garment seamstress and one in the fried pork rind factory.

OUR WHOLE BLOCK would go to Coney Island together. One sweaty, hot subway car. Those were the days of boom boxes, so you'd yell out, "Change the channel! Change the channel!"

CENTRAL PARK, it's beautiful, but you go there and it's so vast. And you don't know anyone.

THAT'S WHY I moved back.

PEOPLE FAULT ME and Spike for opening our big mouths about Brooklyn. We should have kept them shut!

WHEN MY MOTHER put me in the system, I had to be in a convent with nuns. And while I was there, I was dreaming of home. Brooklyn was where my happiness was.

THE NUNS put on plays and they always put me in the lead part.

IT NEVER OCCURRED to me as a career choice—until the day I met Spike Lee in a nightclub. He said, "You're an actress," and I said, "No, I'm not."

BUT, OH MY GOD, the nuns knew.

WHEN I FIRST went to the Barclays Center, I saw every color of the rainbow. It wasn't all whitewashed. It was kids from the neighborhood. One of them said, "Ms. Perez, are you OK?" I said, "Where are you from?" The guy goes, "Well, I live in East Flatbush. My family's been there for years." And I just started bawling.

TO ME, it's a beautiful thing that I've come full circle and I'm still living here. I'm still living within my happiness in my Brooklyn.

MY CUP runneth over. It's just been too good.

BRANDON STANTON

PHOTOGRAPHER AND BLOGGER

I'VE BEEN interviewing people for *Humans of New York* since 2011.

A LOT OF people say no. It took a long time to learn not to internalize that.

WHEN SOMEONE walks up to you, a stranger, a blank slate— no opinion, no judgement— then you are able to share your thoughts with more abandon.

WHAT'S YOUR biggest fear? What's the biggest mistake you've ever made? What do you feel most guilty about?

I'M AWARE of how uncomfortable it is. It's terrifying.

THE FEELING OF being heard is always stronger than the fear of being revealed.

IT'S NOT ABOUT what I say. It's about the energy that I'm giving off.

AND IT'S 10 times easier on 60-degree days.

IT'S NOT VERY systematic. I don't have a spreadsheet.

NORMALLY I'LL DECIDE where to go five minutes before I walk out of my apartment.

I BASICALLY WILL just get off at a train stop.

BED-STUY WAS the very first place I ever went to when I came to New York. It's such a tidal pool where so many different cultures are converging.

I DID A lot of photographing on Fulton Street.

I HAVE INFLUENCE as a storyteller. But I have a healthy feeling that everything on the internet is ephemeral.

NEW YORK CITY feels like a small town to me.

THOUSANDS OF PEOPLE have told me the deepest stories of their life. It can't help but open your mind and make you a more accepting person.

AMETHYST VALENTINO

KARAOKE HOST, ACTRESS

I STARTED HOSTING karaoke at Montero's about 13 years ago.

AT FIRST IT WAS just Fridays, then Friday and Saturday. Now I'm there three nights a week.

FIRST THING YOU see is the fluorescent sign outside, Montero Bar. Right on the corner of Atlantic and Hicks, next to I-278, two blocks from Brooklyn Bridge Park near the water.

IT'S AN OLD longshoremen bar. Been there since 1947.

YOU SEE ALL these old-fashioned life preservers, ships, this beautiful mermaid that used to be part of a ship.

MY ORDER: HENNESSY on the rocks. How can you be in a sailor bar without drinking some whiskey or cognac?

THE REGULARS, we get lawyers, teachers, firemen, politicians.

I HAVE SOME celebrities that pop in now and again. I won't say who.

THEY COME IN, they have fun, and they don't have to worry about being bombarded.

LIVE AND LET LIVE, you know?

I LOVE MY job. I like helping people sing too. Once I've heard them sing, sometimes I'll give them songs I think they would sing well. They appreciate that.

MOST KARAOKE PLACES can change the key up or down. If there is a song you always wanted to try but it's too high, I can put it down.

THEY DON'T KNOW that they're going to have a problem until the bridge, which is the highest part usually.

"ALONE" BY HEART is my song. "Purple Rain," that's another one people like to ask me to sing.

I'M THERE FROM 8:30 to 1:30. But don't come in at 1:00 thinking you're going to sing.

MY MOTTO IS: Make Montero's your first stop, not your last.

MARTY MARKOWITZ

FORMER BOROUGH PRESIDENT

THE BROOKLYN where I grew up was *Father Knows Best*.

WE RODE bicycles. We played stickball. We made scooters out of milk cartons. We would play skully with soda caps.

I LIVED TWO and a half blocks from Ebbets Field.

MY FATHER WAS a waiter in a kosher delicatessen. He died when I was nine.

MY MOTHER WAS a horrible cook. I hate to say that, but it's true. When I got my first taste of Italian food, I fell in love.

JUNIOR'S WILL always be my favorite restaurant.

JFK WAS THE first campaign that I was really involved in. I was 15 when he ran for president, and I was a high school coordinator.

THE ATLANTIC YARDS debate was a very contentious time. The threats, the hostility.

I CAN'T TELL you how many ups and downs we had. People felt that I was a bum, a crook. It didn't make sense.

WHY WOULD I do anything to harm Brooklyn?

I WENT INTO public service to put a smile on everyone's face.

SEPTEMBER 11 was primary day, so I was out in front of a school in Prospect Heights giving out leaflets, and then I heard a thud.

THEN THE second plane hit. I immediately called my wife.

WHO DO I know in that building? Who do we know? Who do we know? Who do we know?

I NEVER WANTED to live in Manhattan. That doesn't mean that it's not exciting and pulsating. It is! You got everything there, let's face it.

BUT THERE'S JUST something about Brooklyn.

MIKE FADEM

RESTAURANT OWNER

WE STARTED WITH the dough.

WHEN WE DEVELOPED the pizza at Ops, I learned how to make, basically, a really good bread that we were just turning into pizza.

I MANAGED restaurants for years, and I'd always dreamed about having my own place.

I WANTED A neighborhood wine bar, somewhere people could come and have a glass of wine that maybe turned into a meal.

MY GOOD FRIEND Gavin, who owns Variety Coffee Roasters, called me and was like, "I know you want to do this pizza thing. Do you want to open this restaurant with me next to my coffee shop?"

THE REST is history.

WE LITERALLY had no idea what we were doing when we started.

LUCKILY, PEOPLE just love pizza. You make one from fresh bread with cheese on it, everybody's happy.

WE DID SO MANY tests. Every week we were doing something different.

WE LANDED ON one that we really liked and figured out a way to make it stable, if not perfectly consistent.

IT'S STILL A wild thing; it's changing all the time, of course. But we have a method now.

I WANTED TO challenge the ideas that were making the restaurants I was working at unavailable to the majority of people, cost-wise. I really wanted Ops to be inviting to everyone.

SOMETIMES I JUST want to cry when I think about how we're all doing this thing that we love, and the fact that it touches people, especially the kind of people who are in an industry where they have to be in restaurants and writing about them all the time.

WHENEVER ANY PRESS comes out, I'm just like, "Holy crap. That's so cool." I pinch myself.

CHRISTIE CHOW

SCHOOL DIRECTOR OF OPERATIONS

IN A MIDDLE school, you have a staff of about 40, you have 350 kids, you have 350 families.

I WAS THE director of operations at Kings Collegiate Charter School for about 10 years.

EACH DAY, you're blocking and tackling as much as you can.

A KID throws up. A parent calls with a question. A bus breaks down. You take away distractions and pain points so that the teachers can teach.

A SAFE ENVIRONMENT does so much for creating real, even unlikely, friendships.

STRUCTURE LETS a kid be a kid. Leave them alone and kids can get lost in the shuffle.

I LIVED IN Hell's Kitchen when I started, so to get to work, my wakeup was 3:45 a.m. That's one reason why I moved to Brooklyn.

LEAVING THE SCHOOL was a really, really hard decision.

YOU WORK HARD to shape the staff into what you want it to be, the culture of your school.

THERE'S SO MUCH responsibility with that role, but there's also so much satisfaction: All the decisions that you make, you see that immediate impact.

I WORK FOR a network of over 50 charter schools, K-12. The vision is for all students to have the opportunity to enroll and graduate from college.

NOW I'M A senior project manager on the operations team of the home office.

IN THIS POSITION, I had the opportunity to take the experience I had and start to learn a totally different skill set, while still implementing all of the things that I learned as a director of operations. I'm able to influence in the same ways, but on a grander scale.

I STILL desperately miss being at a school every day.

JOSEPH VOLPICELLI

BARBER

I CAME HERE in 1956 from Italy, and I came to work in Park Slope in 1961 and here we are. Still.

THE ITALIAN, it's always there. Nobody could take that away. Nobody!

NO! I NEVER lived in Park Slope. I lived in Bensonhurst until 1982, and then in Manhattan Beach for 33 years!

I WAS 16, and we took a ship to America, the *Andrea Doria*. Two months after our trip, the *Andrea Doria* sank near Cape Cod. It was like we'd lost a family member.

PARK SLOPE back then, you would see signs on the cars saying, "Please don't break the glass, there's nothing in the car."

YOU COULD BUY a brownstone for $30,000.

NOW THESE NEW people from all over the country, they hear Park Slope, Park Slope, Park Slope. Boom.

ALL OF A SUDDEN Brooklyn is a brand!

THERE'S NOT REALLY anything to miss other than the people. Unfortunately, they're gone to live somewhere else or they're gone [points up to the sky].

THE LADY IN the first chair, Charmaine, she's been here 30 years. Lana's been here 19 years. Alex was a young kid when he first came, now he has six boys. Susan's here 11 years.

IN THE MID-'70S, when everybody with the long hair, business was very bad. Nobody around here was getting a haircut.

MY GRANDDAUGHTER, the younger one, she calls me Nonno.

"NONNO, MY BANGS are getting too long!" she says.

WHO OTHER THAN a doctor touches your head the first time that you meet the person?

JO FIRESTONE

COMEDIAN

TO LIVE IN Brooklyn, there are sacrifices that have to be made.

ALL OF THE sewage from the whole block backed up into our apartment. Also I think there's a spider infestation.

IT'S THE BEST apartment I've ever lived in—apart from the poop and the spiders.

I THINK THE funniest moments are the most unexpected ones.

WHEN I THINK about bad things that happen and find humor in it, it feels like I have more control.

I GET A LOT of material from being dumped.

MY MOM IS the funniest person in our family, only she doesn't know it.

YOU THINK THAT something will be funny and you try it out.

IT'S THE CHAOS. That's the whole thrill.

WHEN IT WORKS, when the audience is jumping on every word, when you can barely get them out fast enough, when they seem to cherish them in a way only laughter can show— it feels pretty awesome.

THE WORLD'S TINIEST Comedy Club was an installation I did in Manhattan with dolls and miniature stuff. People could come in and do their stand-up.

THERE ARE LOTS of people in New York who are down for weird shit.

IT TAKES A certain amount of presence to laugh. You have to really be there before you can let loose.

I USUALLY JUST have a kernel of an idea and I flesh it out with the audience. I want to get on stage as soon as possible.

IF YOU LET an idea sit too long, you start to have doubts and that's poison.

SAWAKO OKOCHI

CHEF

I WAS a picky eater.

AS A CHILD, I was always left alone at the dinner table. Sometimes I'd sit there for an hour looking at my plate.

WE MOVED TO Texas from Japan.

SCHOOL FOOD was a big disappointment. That led me to start cooking on my own.

I DECIDED to go to culinary school in New York. Everything about the city was surprising—dirty streets and subways, and everybody walked. I got tired a lot.

WHEN MY HUSBAND I started dating, we were both unemployed. We spent the whole summer hanging out.

ONE DAY he was at the Brooklyn library looking at archives of old Jewish restaurants, and he came across a place called Shalom Japan. The name stayed with us.

WE KNEW it'd be hard.

NORMAL DAYS, I check inventory on pastry first and make what's needed. Then I test recipes with Aaron and help the cooks if needed. We have a staff meal, then daily meeting and go into service.

WHO WOULD THINK about putting a lox bowl with sushi rice?

SAKE KASU CHALLAH. Toro toasts with scallion cream cheese. Mochi ice cream blintzes. And Aaron's matzoh ramen.

FOOD MAKES people happy.

YOU GET AN OLD Brooklyn feel in South Williamsburg. We live above the restaurant.

WHEN I WAS back in Japan, my dad took me took a restaurant by the ocean that served sea urchin and squid over rice with egg yolk in the center. It's the best thing ever.

I WANT to eat that before I die.

ANDY HUNTER

BOOK PUBLISHER

I WANTED TO go to an MFA to immerse myself in a community of writers that had my interests. I had sort of a romantic vision of what that would mean.

AT BROOKLYN COLLEGE, I became the editor in chief of *The Brooklyn Review*, which had a print run of 600 copies.

I WAS SHOCKED and dismayed at how little reach there was for literary magazines.

I STARTED *Electric Literature* in 2009 with Scott Lindenbaum, who I met at Brooklyn College.

THE IDEA WAS to take all the lessons I had learned from more commercial magazine publishing and apply them to a literary magazine.

THE STUFF THAT was revolutionary about *Electric Lit* is completely commonplace now.

THE FACT THAT we published in all formats, in audio and e-books. That we included multimedia.

That we had a huge social media presence.

CATAPULT AND LIT HUB both came out of people who admired *Electric Lit*, who came to me and had some ideas, and I decided to collaborate with them.

EVERY ONE OF these things has been an attempt to fill some kind of gap or to support the culture I've dedicated my life to—the culture around books and writing.

AN INDUSTRY THAT was $18 billion in 2009 is now a $9 billion industry because the other $9 billion went to Amazon.

BOOKSHOP.ORG is my indie, scrappy attempt to offset that and to make sure that bookstores that don't have resources can try to compete with Amazon.

IT'S ALL ABOUT trying to reinforce the key components of the culture I love and keep it healthy.

I DON'T KNOW if it's enough. But it's what we can do.

EDWIDGE DANTICAT

WRITER

IN HAITI, whenever someone said they were going to the United States, they would say they were going to New York.

MY IDEA of Brooklyn, though, was of the cold place where my parents lived.

WE SPOKE TO our parents every Sunday from a phone booth in downtown Port-au-Prince and tried to catch them up on our lives.

I CAME TO New York when I was 12. It was a great shock. I remember looking down from the airplane and seeing New York City below. It was so huge and full of lights.

I'M GOING to have so much to do here, I thought.

IN MY childhood mind, I imagined that my life would be touched by each and every one of those lights.

WHEN I WALKED down the hallway in our building in East Flatbush, every door was closed. I remember being struck by that. Why would they keep their door locked? What were they afraid of?

MOST OF the people were Haitian, or from some other part of the Caribbean.

THE FIRST BOOK I ever owned was Ludwig Bemelmans' *Madeline*. My uncle gave it to me. I remember holding that book in my hand and thinking, This is what I want to do.

I WANTED TO tell a story that people didn't have to speak aloud, a story that they could hold in their hands.

MY FATHER was what was then called a "gypsy cab" driver. I got to see a lot of Brooklyn that way.

AN AIRPORT TRIP was a gold mine.

AFTER MY first novel, *Breath, Eyes, Memory,* was selected for Oprah Winfrey's book club, my dad told me, "Well, now you

have enough money for medical school."

....

WHEN I FIRST saw my parents' tax return, as I was applying for college, I was shocked. How had they raised four children on that? I wondered.

MY PARENTS are both gone now. But it was their courage and sacrifice that made possible the lives we now live. I owe everything to the trip they took to Brooklyn.

....

IT WAS A leap of faith.

STORIES

_Essays and selected writing
from noted Brooklyn voices_

THE PARAKEET

Written by **MARIE-HELENE BERTINO** | **ONCE UPON A TIME** a cargo ship unloading in the Brooklyn Navy Yard dropped a crate that cracked in two and exploded into thousands of green-and-lemon parakeets. Some built homes in the spires of Brooklyn College. Some nested in the mausoleums of Green-Wood Cemetery, enjoying its startling views of the harbor and the Statue of Liberty.

Absolutely no one in Green-Wood Cemetery is trying to be anything they're not. They're dead—no talking them out of it. This is one of the reasons I decided to run its periphery after years of running Prospect Park. The park had begun to depress me. Having only three months of good weather translates into enormous pressure to be outside when it's warm—using nature as your treadmill, hurling plastic objects across the meadow, spreading an artisan cheese across a roll. One day the activities seemed dishonest, the people under duress, not letting on how maybe they'd rather be inside with the shades drawn, staring off.

Green-Wood Cemetery has a more acceptable ratio of truth to beauty. Its perimeter is 3.5 miles and its flora is abundant and fragrant. Even when I'm running through one of the more disparate sections, when it's just me, sidewalk trash and a few braked big rigs whose drivers are conked out in naps, the smell of lilac emanates from inside the gates. Trash and lilac is a dynamic that makes sense to me.

The parakeets are resourceful, accidental immigrants. They roost in utility pole transformers that warm them during Brooklyn's frigid winters, causing innumerable problems for Con Edison. Their stick nests are complicated interconnected series of apartments with separate entrances and garages. Hard to relocate.

I see the parakeets when I run. Arcing out over the hills, or perched in trees overlooking mourners, fanned amidst the branches like a colorful firework.

I live in a Brooklyn neighborhood called Windsor Terrace that is bordered by Green-Wood Cemetery on the west, Prospect Park on the east. The folks who live here have nicknamed it "Old Brooklyn" because many of them have owned their homes for over 50 years. Fifty years is considered a long time in America. I moved to the neighborhood to have a quiet place to write my speculative fiction stories.

Sound had been the major feature of my previous neighborhood in Queens. My apartment had been situated under the elevated 7 train, next to the Long Island Railroad, and beneath the flight patterns of two international airports. Every 10 minutes the express train shook the wine glasses in our cabinet. A halal meat cart company's headquarters was in our basement. They'd haul their heavy carts past our bedroom window precisely at 6:30 a.m. every morning.

Our wine glasses, our bedroom window. Which had become my glasses, my bedroom window. During the aftermath of a seminal breakup, untrue friends shuddered away from me like bones shed meat in boiling water. My life had become the sound of metal scraping against unrelenting concrete. I began to feel like a photocopy of myself.

When a friend was leaving her apartment on East 4th Street in Windsor Terrace, she asked if I'd like to take over the lease. I packed my wine glasses and my two cats, and I moved.

In April of 1912, in a French village so scant it does not qualify for maps, my great-grandmother fell in love with a gypsy boy and became pregnant. Concerned she would disgrace the family, her father banished her, buying her a third-class ticket on a ship that was sailing for America. My great-grandmother was 18 years old. Her name was Jeanne. Her father's name was Baptiste. The village's name was Gazave, and it was built into the foothills of the Pyrenees Mountains. I don't know what the gypsy boy's name was. The ship would leave from Cherbourg, France, on April 10th, and take 15 days to scoot across the Atlantic Ocean before arriving at Ellis Island in New York.

The backyards of East 4th Street butt up against the backyards of East 3rd Street. From my second-floor window, I can see no fewer than 10 of them. Some yards are meticulously organized into what is plant life and what is a table and chairs. Some, like ours, are overtaken by evergreen trees. All of the yards comprise a busy avenue for animals crossing from either the park to the cemetery or vice versa. I imagine a bird gathering twigs in the park, then flying over our yards to its cemetery pad. A raccoon with an elegant suitcase. A squirrel hoisting a hobo bag over its shoulder. It is a dangerous journey due to the dogs of Brooklyn, tied and watchful in our backyards, who have been known to thrash a possum or stray cat.

When I was growing up, my family had several dogs and cats but the first pet that was solely mine was a green-and-yellow parakeet I named Micky after my favorite member of The Monkees. Micky was mine to feed and groom and clean and maintain, a prospect that, at nine years old, I was too young to be terrified by.

Micky and I spent many happy afternoons together. I would read and he'd sit on his perch and sing or make the gravelly, garbled sound I considered a secret between us. I read every parakeet book I could find and memorized several facts. Parakeets have a third eyelid. Parakeets have monocular vision, which means they use each eye independently. They can turn their heads 180 degrees because they have more neck vertebrae than humans.

I loved Micky, even though he figure-eighted away whenever I tried to pet his velvet, avocado-colored forehead, which is called a crown eye.

One day, I decided Micky was a vegetarian, like my mom. I replaced the seeds in his feeding dish with chopped up carrots and lettuce. He didn't seem to like them, but I knew with time he'd get used to it. Days went by, then weeks. I assumed he would eat when he got hungry enough. I didn't notice when he stopped singing. I found him at the bottom of the cage, stiff and heavy. The first time I'd ever seen something dead.

After that I mistrusted myself as a caretaker. I never again wanted to be the only thing standing between a living thing and death.

Something happened that changed their minds.

Maybe the gypsy was begging to see Jeanne, or she him, or perhaps Baptiste realized they couldn't wait that long to ship my great-grandmother away from France. For whatever reason, Jeanne needed to get gone sooner. So Baptiste bought another ticket for

a different ship that would leave on April 4th, six days before the original ship. They took the train to Le Havre and my grandmother boarded the SS *Niagara* on April 4th, 1912. Did she have morning sickness? Did she look back as she crossed the gangway or did she stare stubbornly forward? I don't know any of these things.

I know she was at sea for 11 days. I know that on April 10th, the day she had originally planned to leave, the SS *Niagara* hit ice off the coast of Newfoundland. The collision dented the bow plates and the ship began to leak. The crew sent off an SOS. signal, which at the time was a relatively new way of asking for help. A nearby ship rushed to aid, but the SS *Niagara* crew was able to repair the damage themselves. Everything went back to normal. The ship continued on.

Four days later, the ship my great-grandmother was supposed to take, the RMS *Titanic,* would hit the same ice off the coast of Newfoundland. The captain would be rendered paralyzed by indecision, the life boats would be lowered without being even half filled, and the ship would sink with most of its third-class passengers trapped below deck.

Imagine the relocations that spiraled out of that mistake.

Windsor Terrace's local shelter has a constantly evolving menagerie of animals found on the street or surrendered by unwilling or incapable owners or pulled from their wild lives in Prospect Park. The shelter and its supply store are run by a man named Sean Casey. He rarely speaks to me even though I'm there several times a week, carrying teetering stacks of cans to the checkout, or asking if any dogs need walking. He is a neighborhood celebrity who has rehabilitated and found homes for countless animals, infiltrated fighting rings and freed all the dogs chained to the walls. His exploits are documented on the shelter's blog.

One week Sean camped out on the Brooklyn railroad, tracking a pair of wild pit bulls that had been attacking local dogs. The pit bulls lived in a hovel no one could find and had outsmarted several teams from the SPCA. Sean spent a week living and thinking like the wild dogs, until one night he caught the duo's male member. The bitch continued to elude him. Every night she'd bay and howl, heartbroken and calling for her mate.

The neighborhood felt a surprising amount pity for this hurt creature that almost overrode the horror we felt for the dogs she had attacked. Every day we checked the blog to see if she had been caught. One day a picture was posted of Sean standing next to a chocolate-colored pit bull who seemed too puny to be causing such ruckus.

That's when we realized we had hoped she'd stay free forever. Or at least I had.

Speculative fiction is sometimes called fabulism, lumped under the umbrella term of magic realism. There are as many different ways of defining it as there are writers and readers. In a classical magic realist story, the dead walk freely among the living and flying things can symbolize the transition a character makes from one social class to another, from one world to the next, or from the land of the living to the land of the dead. An indicator that you are within the realm of speculative fiction is that something happens that does not obey the laws of physics. It is not unusual for someone to turn into a bird or a butterfly.

A few years ago, I went to the animal shelter to buy cat food. Bending to reach a particular can, I noticed a dainty cage under a pile of empty crates. I peered inside and found a tiny dog with enormous ears, sitting politely on a spread of newspaper. His quivering brown eyes reminded me of my grandmother's and he looked like a miniature fox. Sean told me he was a Papillon who had just been surrendered. His owner was moving to an apartment that didn't allow animals. So here he was, shivering in a cage.

Papillon, I said. The French word for butterfly.

My apartment, a one bedroom with two cats and no washer and dryer, was not suitable for a dog. However, I adopted him, for two reasons. The first was that I thought my grandmother had sent him to me. The second was that I missed her and having a family so much it had become an ache I had to pull aside to do everyday things like errands, the way you pull aside a curtain to enter the bath.

I imagine my great-grandmother on that enormous ship staring out of a porthole and panicking. Then I pluck her off the SS *Niagara* and place her onto the lower decks of the *Titanic*, where she would have been locked behind partitions along with the other non-English-speaking third-class passengers. In addition to social reasons, this was so the immigrants could access Ellis Island from a different entrance where they could be questioned and documented. Fewer than half of the third-class women on the *Titanic* survived. It is likely that Jeanne would have perished, along with my grandmother, who was growing inside of her.

SHE HAD ALWAYS FELT DIFFERENT THAN THE REST OF HER FAMILY. THIS EXPLAINED WHY.

But they didn't perish. When the SS *Niagara* delivered my great-grandmother safely to Ellis Island on April 15th, 1912, the clerk asked her two questions. They were the same two questions they asked every immigrant because someone official had decided that useful things could be gleaned about a large swath of people by how they answered them.

Can you read?

Can you write?

Her answers are recorded on the ship's manifest.

Yes.

Yes.

Jeanne traveled to the boarding house where other people from Gazave had settled. There she met the gypsy's brother, Pierre, the white sheep of the family. They married. It was the early 1900s, when people still had secrets and the world was small enough for coincidences. That October Jeanne gave birth to my grandmother, and Pierre raised his brother's daughter as his own.

When my grandmother was 65 years old, Jeanne told her that the man she thought was her father was actually her uncle. Her father was the gypsy, not the white sheep. My grandmother said this revelation was and was not a surprise. She had always felt different from the rest of her family. This explained why.

Relocating is traumatic. It can cause a dog to be abandoned in a cage. It can lead to a studio apartment with possums in the backyard, a running habit. It can maroon exotic birds in a land with an unfriendly climate.

Last week a parakeet sat in a patch of grass inside the Green-Wood Cemetery gate, watching me as I went running by. I slowed and halted in front of it. It side-eyed me with interest.

Hello, bird, I said.

It did not answer but allowed me to admire it. The smart tufts of lime-green feathers like a hat, its regal nape and mantle. Parakeets are twitchy, afraid of what's above and behind them. Obsessive-compulsive, they perform every movement several times.

Are you enjoying the winter?

It shrugged and shrugged and shrugged. *I like the quiet.*

Does it make you feel isolated?

Whenever I can I can fly to Coney Island, to the Cloisters, to Queens. I can see all the way to Mexico.

But don't you get lonely?

I am far from alone, it said, blinking and blinking and blinking.

I looked up and the trees were filled with birds. Red-throated, blue-billed, speckled-tailed something-or-others. An array of parakeets blinked amidst the branches like a yellow-and-green constellation.

I live between a park and a cemetery, but which is which might surprise you. Every October the park dies, while the cemetery teems with life.

Parakeets have anxiety but they are not afraid of death. They sleep inside of death. They nuzzle between the shoulder blades of a stone angel, in the corners of crypts, or the cracked-out shelf of a mausoleum.

Parakeets do not engage in debates about social media on social media. They do not reveal their political views and think most people are overrated. They have ambivalent feelings about the term "unofficial mascot of Brooklyn College." They have soft underbellies and have lost almost all of their Spanish, which is a shame, but gets filed under *things we shed to belong*.

Certainly we can assume there are nights when they're homesick for Argentina. When they fly to the top of the highest spire at Green-Wood Cemetery and gaze at the ships crisscrossing the harbor.

I'm not from Brooklyn, either. Like the parakeets, my great-grandmother and, it figures, I, are here because someone made a mistake. Like the parakeets, my people are nomadic and nervous. But I stay and stay and stay, even when the cold feels like nails scraping against my DNA echo. I walk my dog. I run the same terrain over and over to get strong. When I feel lonely, I drive to Valentino Pier and watch the ships. I'm no longer scared to be the only thing between a living creature and death. My husband says this is because I'm more maternal than I allow myself to believe. I mother everything, he says. Him, our animals, our friends, strangers, ideas of things. I feather our nest in Brooklyn's unfriendly winters so we stay warm. I keep a cheerful color. I am a parakeet.

MARIE-HELENE BERTINO is the author of the novels *2 A.M. at the Cat's Pajamas* and *Parakeet* and the story collection *Safe as Houses*.

THE CIRCLE PARK

Written by **LATONYA YVETTE** | On a double-laned two-way street, past Bishop's purple high school, over the wiggly grate that trips my vintage cruiser. Up over the hill, past bustling Atlantic Avenue, and further than Dean Street and the ice cream shop with its own churner that was sold last summer. By the bookshop with the backyard, near the four-chair Dominican salon that burned my scalp at 13, and even closer to Mayday, a hardware store that opened in 1964, two years before my mother was born, the store my grandmother dragged me into for bits and bobs, door plates, fasteners and old knobs, or plain good Brooklyn conversation. Beyond all this sits what my family has always called the "circle park."

For generations, Dr. Ronald McNair Park [formerly Guider Park] has been quietly tucked between the expanse of the Brooklyn Botanic Garden and the stately Prospect Heights High School. At first glance, it is just a typical New York City park, with forest-green benches peppering the edges. It doesn't offer a playground or beloved splash pad, but the trees bloom in the spring, fill out in the summer, and hibernate in the winter, as they do everywhere. Otherwise, the park appears unromantic, undramatic—and, quite possibly, unappealing, to the untrained eye.

In 2018, an average of 30,000 pedestrians and 3,000 bicyclists crossed the Brooklyn Bridge each day. Maybe they took photos under the Brooklyn Bridge, hopped on the ferry from DUMBO to North Williamsburg, dined in Red Hook or walked along the Gowanus Canal. I wonder how many visitors allowed themselves to feel the coruscating pull of Dr. Ronald McNair Park.

McNair was a man, who, by chance, shared his name with my uncle, my grandfather and my great-grandfather. I did not know him, but I knew him as a figure in the place I knew best. Dr. McNair taught karate and was a celebrated saxophonist before becoming America's second Black astronaut to travel to space. In 1986, McNair was one of seven astronauts who lifted off in the *Challenger* from Cape Canaveral, Florida. Within 73 seconds, the shuttle was engulfed in smoke—what looked like an explosion—and eventually the *Challenger* and all seven of its crew plummeted into the Atlantic at a speed of nearly 200 miles per hour.

There are several hypotheses for why the accident happened the way it did. But today, what I mostly wonder about is how McNair's life shaped mine and those of other Brooklyn-born Black kids. He was 35 when he died, three years before my mother had me. Did his body feel held as he felt a unique kind of freeness that would only be offered to a Black man shooting beyond space and time? What would he have told us about his adventure? And would my park, our park, the circle park, still be salient for those of us who know it well?

Now, three decades have passed since his death, and two since my childhood days dancing in that park at 10, under the sticky Brooklyn sun, and I'm raising two of my own tiny New Yorkers. As we move through our New York City home, I come across these intersections of history and personal experience, stories that travel on us and with us through space, told by generations of Black folk I only know from penny-colored statues and trees with plaques. Nevertheless, while I marvel at what has been carefully given to me, I hold to the task of writing my own stories at the feet of their grand and collective memories. So that I may continue to press on in this magnitude, in this life. When my grandmother spent her days in the circle park reading, planning, dreaming and praying, she may have felt connected to Ronald McNair: rocketing off into space, defying gravity and norms. Or maybe he was just a statue in a park where she daydreamed her own adventures.

Right next to the circle park, tourists snap selfies in front of the giant spouts of water that burst on timers outside of the Brooklyn Museum. On good days, my children run barefoot through the spray as I sip coffee on the concrete steps, and they become little curly-headed dots. They float past the botanical garden, with its thousand trees and gardens of magnolias and roses. They run by Mount Prospect Park and the Central Library, a meeting place for both learning and activism. Nearby, the Soldiers' and Sailors' Arch of Grand Army Plaza stands, attractive and fierce.

I spent my summers in the midst of these monuments, too, and back then, just like for my children, it was just summertime fun. I wonder if, as locals, we do our due diligence, appropriately basking in the wonder. I wonder if my mother or grandmother thought the same, watching me dance in the circle park, thinking about Black astronauts.

For generations, that park has been a meeting place for my family. I imagine it is a center of solace and safety for other Black folk and people of color in the community, protected, in a sense, by a four-point intersection and several plots of grass. There have been protests in the surrounding area to protect tenants from rapid gentrification—a kind of gentrification that, among many things, puts the park's unmarred beauty and centrality at risk.

Sometimes, I dream of myself as an elder in that same park: a kindly older woman who remembers the blood-stained cement to the right of McNair's monument, where, when she was a girl, she skinned her knee while skipping and was told to "Get back up!" Hopefully, she'll remember the rollerblade skids she etched on that same sidewalk, and the exact bench where she devoured brown paper bags of corner-store Swedish Fish and Swiss Rolls. She'll remember where she took her kids one evening to celebrate the legacy of her own grandmother— their great-grandmother—with their grandmother, at her favorite bench. It was October, in those same plots of grass below Dr. Ronald McNair's rocket ship-shaped statue.

Someday, I'll be her. For now, I'm a woman who remembers growing up in the circle park. I'm a mother who takes her own children there, where they squish their toes in the grass. I understand the immensity of this small park's history, but I cherish writing my own story here too. In this city, there is excitement and ceremony and plenty to photograph, but to me, there is nothing more New York than sitting on a bench, in a little park, sandwiched between here and there, between the known and unknown, finding a place of your own as the city spins around you.

LATONYA YVETTE is a Brooklyn-based writer, creative and founder of LY, an eponymous lifestyle site focused on style, motherhood, wellbeing and more. Her first book, *Woman Of Color*, was published in 2019. Her second book is set to be published by Dial Press in fall 2022.

SHELFTALKER

Written by **EMMA STRAUB**

PART I: 2014

The staff at BOOKCOURT is both good-looking and well-read, the books are well displayed, and the children's section is appropriately in its own little nook, perfect for whiling away the hours. Singles say the store is excellent for date browsing as well.

I wrote that blurb for *The Village Voice*'s Best of New York issue in 2005, four years before I started working at the bookstore. It's a little bit like calling my older self good-looking [thank you, younger self], but more than that, I feel like it's proof that the store and I were always meant to be. When I wrote the blurb, I lived a few blocks away, having just moved in with my then-boyfriend [now husband], and we would often amble the aisles before or after dinner in Cobble Hill. I meant every word, except for the date browsing, which I'd completely made up, based on the fact that the owner's young son Zack [younger than me by a few years, then in his early twenties] was a gorgeous flirt with dark hair and bright blue eyes, and every heterosexual woman I knew in the neighborhood wanted to sleep with him.

BookCourt opened in 1981, when Henry Zook and Mary Gannett were just a couple of kids, both only 27 years old. I love to think about what they were like then—the high rounds of her cheeks, his broad shoulders—and wonder what they imagined the future might hold for them and their little store. It's so easy to look at the neighborhood and to see the bookstore—spacious, light, crowded with well-dressed starlets—as a given, but it certainly wasn't. Is there any greater piece of advice in New York City retail than to buy the building? Henry and Mary bought the building.

The store takes up two storefronts on Court Street, in what is now prime Cobble Hill retail territory—there is a Rag and Bone shop across the street, the kind of clothing store with low lighting and one leather jacket hanging in the window, and a James Perse expensive t-shirt store down the block. A Barney's CO-OP—the only one in Brooklyn—is around the corner. A couple of years ago, there was great consternation at the bookstore when it was revealed that J.Crew was planning to take over the deli on the corner where the staff often ran to buy mid-shift bottles of water and gummi bears. Thankfully, the gummi bears remain in place, at least for now.

When I was in high school, about 10 blocks away from the store's front door, the neighborhood was full of old Italian ladies making mozzarella and Middle Eastern spice shops along Atlantic Avenue. When my male friends would walk through late at night, they worried about boys with baseball bats, a threat that always seemed like something out of a previous century, or maybe a movie musical. I never went to BookCourt as a teenager—I commuted to Brooklyn from Manhattan's Upper West Side, and I never stayed in Brooklyn after school unless I was going to a friend's house. Even if I had visited, it wouldn't have been the same shop that exists now—for the first 15 years of its life, BookCourt occupied a single storefront with a basement, which I would guess maxed out at about 700 square feet. In 1996, when I was a sophomore in high school, Henry and Mary bought the building next door, and expanded the store into the space that had previously been a flower shop, which added another 400 square feet or so. That was the incarnation of the store that I wrote about for *The Village Voice*, cozy and densely packed. In 2008, they built a giant addition onto the back of the flower shop space—the Greenhouse, they called it, because the room was where a greenhouse for the flower shop had once stood—tripling their square footage. A Barnes & Noble had recently opened a few blocks down Court Street. BookCourt was doubling down—they knew what people in the neighborhood wanted: a beautiful space filled with a curated selection of books. Places to sit. No coffee, no Wi-Fi. It was a middle finger to the idea of the corporate giant—they were staying put, and getting bigger. The Greenhouse was [and remains] studded with skylights, with a high ceiling, and walking into it feels like a magic wormhole straight to California.

I started working at BookCourt in 2009, just after I returned home to New York City after graduate school. I knew Zack a bit, and we'd been

in touch about setting up an event I was doing at the store for a small book of mine, a single short story that was charitably being published by a small press as a novella. I was looking for a job—any job—on Craigslist, and there it was, a posting for a bookseller gig at BookCourt. I wrote to Zack immediately, and we scheduled an "interview," which is a very loose word indeed for what transpired. I met Zack at the benches in front of the store's red door, and we went down the stairs at the center of the paperback fiction room, and then we sat down with his father, Henry, also a handsome flirt, who was wearing his running clothes. I would soon learn that Henry was usually wearing his running clothes. [For sartorial fairness, I should add that Mary is most often found in a sky-blue cardigan that matches her eyes, which are even brighter and prettier than her son's.]

> **IT'S SO EASY TO LOOK AT THE NEIGHBOR-HOOD AND TO SEE THE BOOKSTORE—SPACIOUS, LIGHT, CROWDED WITH WELL-DRESSED STAR-LETS—AS A GIVEN, BUT IT CERTAINLY WASN'T.**

I had my book party for the little novella on a Sunday night, and started working at 9 a.m. the next day. My book—all 27 pages of it—was that week's number 1 fiction bestseller. No one on the staff could have cared less. Everyone wanted to talk about Roberto Bolaño's early work, or John Williams' *Stoner*, or Barry Hannah's *Airships*, or, even more so, who else on staff they wanted to sleep with. I fell in love with the job immediately, the way some people feel about cocaine or SoulCycle. How had I survived so long without this particular pleasure?

Any long-standing retail establishment that sells culture is going to be staffed by a motley crew of opinionated weirdos, and BookCourt is no exception. The staff is big—maybe 15 people, almost all of whom work part-time, for less money than I now pay my teenage babysitter. In my time, there were always a solid number of recent college grads in cute outfits, the boys with short, tight pants, and the girls in enormous sweaters and mini-dresses that made shelving books a potential peep show. About two-thirds of the staff were PhD students, writers and poets. The rest of the staff were eccentrics, gray-haired and intermittently surly, sometimes in Hawaiian shirts. Anyone who chooses to work the front lines of a shop selling books is going to be both chatty and at least a little bit insane.

We arrived in waves—Chad, Adam, Brisa, Molly, me, Andrew, Maryam. Jack came back after some years away. Glenn, a Brit. Lauren became the new Molly. Christien became the new Chad. Laura and Martha got fired for no reason. Stephen couldn't have been fired if he set the building on fire. Steve, my favorite employee, came to BookCourt from the funeral parlor down the block, where he also did odd jobs. He packed up the cardboard boxes and wore an FDNY fleece and protested for years when the store cat went to go live with Henry after befouling a stroller or two. Nothing was fair or equal. We were lopsided in our talents. Zack handsold the same few books to anyone who asked [Arthur Bradford's *Dogwalker* and Thomas McCarthy's *Remainder*, or a Michel Houellebecq], but I had fallback favorites too [Meg Wolitzer's *The Wife*, Elaine Dundy's *The Dud Avocado*, Donna Tartt's *The Secret History*]. We wrote ecstatic shelftalkers, the little blurbs written by booksellers in our Staff Favorites section, and we rejoiced when someone took our advice and forked over cash for our beloved sentences and paragraphs.

Working for a family business is almost irresistible. Among the staff there were usually half a dozen writers, and we would all joke about it: which one of us would write the sitcom, the short story, the novel inspired by the store's owners, and the rest of us, all of us with our own hilarious storylines. Henry and Mary had split up some years before [I would rather die than ask for more specific details], but continue to run the business together. They get along remarkably well—no worse than any married couple I have ever seen or interacted with in a prolonged way, with no more than an errant eye roll. I know a thousand nominally happy couples whom I regularly see fight far more often and awkwardly. Still, one would occasionally get asked to do something [shelve these books here!] and then asked to do the direct opposite thing [shelve them over there!] by different family members. Staff members spent a lot of time pretending to stare at the ceiling and/or the floor. Zack, a talented photographer, has since moved to the Virgin Islands, where he does lots of things that don't involve working with his parents. We all understand.

In my tenure as a bookseller, I hid behind the counter twice. The first was when Jennifer Egan came in shortly before the publication of *A Visit from the Goon Squad,* and I was too full of love for her to speak. I ducked behind the counter and waited until she was gone to come out. The second time was when a boy I'd hooked up with in high school in particularly gross circumstances [a friend's pullout sofa, very bad oral sex] came in and browsed—the fact that the store was so close to my school was both a boon and a police baton to the knees. On the one hand, it meant that I could handsell copies of my short story collection, published in 2009 by a very, very small press, to every single person I knew. Parents of friends, former teachers, everyone— the print run was 2,000, and I sold 800 of them over the counter at BookCourt. On the other hand, it meant that I often had to make small talk with people I had never liked, such as my friend's stepfather who accused me of stealing something from him in 1995. I didn't.

There were other writers who charmed us all—the drinkers and the storytellers, the nervous, the Irish. One former staff member who was always on drugs walked in on Jonathan Lethem in the bathroom. There were the writers who knew how boring readings could be and instead played Donna Summer on their iPads and did stand-up comedy [Colson Whitehead], and the writers who did the old-fashioned boring reading thing so well that we all wept from the beauty [Colm Tóibín]. Someone passed out when Don DeLillo read, which I assume was because it was too hot and crowded, and not because of the material. Jonathan Franzen endeared himself to me hugely by hurrying to Paula Fox's side at his packed event for *Freedom*—he was clearly so honored and moved to have her there, and made sure she was comfortable. Yes, Jonathan, we all thought, yes, you can stay. [Another favorite to handsell: Paula Fox's *Desperate Characters.*]

Of course, in a beautiful, clean, safe Brooklyn neighborhood, most people are more interested in movie stars than writers, even the booksellers. It's humiliating, the ways in which a bookseller will attempt to have a conversation with a browsing movie star. *I love your yoga mat,* Hope Davis. *Sure is rainy out there,* Paul Giamatti. *I love your overalls,* Emily Mortimer. Paul Dano and Zoe Kazan were our little ringers, our favorites—they bought books all the time. Most of the famous customers were the ones you would assume you would like in real life, whose noses were a little bit funny to be proper leading ladies, who looked like they had messy piles of books on their nightstand. The bad movie stars were the ones who came in with their friends and tried [loudly] to tell them everything that they'd ever read—we loved those the most, because we got to make fun of them the moment they left. I once had to ask poor Natalie Portman for her billing zip code because our credit card machine wasn't functioning properly and she looked at me as if I'd asked for her home address and social security number.

I quit when I was three months pregnant. It was January, post-retail Christmas rush. Anyone who works retail, whether it's books or broomsticks, will tell you what Christmas is like, a zippy blur. Wrapping presents, enormous stacks of books. People will buy whatever you tell them to, so desperate to buy anything. *I need something for my step-grandfather, I need something for a tween, help!* [David McCullough, Rainbow Rowell.] I was down to two shifts a week, and loath to give it up, but my double deadlines were looming—my baby was due in August and my new book was due in September. I was about to go to Mallorca to do research, and it seemed silly to not just quit. I met Mary in her apartment [she lives above the store, of course] to tell her, both about quitting and the reason why, and we both cried.

I'm still in the store every few weeks—my son, now a year and a half old, loves to pull books off the shelves, and will sit and read as I saw thousands of other tiny people sit and read in my tenure. On a recent visit, my son and I were sitting on a sofa in the Greenhouse, reading. A young man—maybe 23 years old, in a cardigan and glasses—was working his second shift. He ducked behind the counter to ask his co-worker how to do something—ah, the keystrokes I've forgotten. I welcomed him to the store, as if it were my place to do so. I didn't tell him that I was a writer, or my name. I just said, "I used to work here. It's nice, isn't it?" He nodded, flustered, wanting to get it all right. He might last six months. He might last six years. I hope the store lasts forever.

PART II: 2021

It is astonishing what a few years can do.

Mike and I sometimes fantasized about taking over for Henry and Mary when they retired. We talked about it from time to time, with the same level of seriousness that we might talk about moving to California someday, or getting in an Airstream trailer and driving across the country. Sounds like fun, but probably won't ever do it.

In 2016, we had just moved back to Cobble Hill. The child who was a toddler when I wrote Part I was now three, and we had a brand-new baby. The four of us were in BookCourt on a late fall afternoon, and the baby was getting fussy, so I took him outside. Steve was there, in his firefighter t-shirt, his face prickly with whiskers. Steve told me that Henry and Mary had sold the building.

I wrote to Henry and Mary that night. *Come over*, Mary said, and we did.

Over the next week, we talked to Henry and Mary about everything—the finances, the business, the costs. We didn't know anything, except this: The neighborhood needed a bookstore, and people were going to be heartbroken. It was October, a few weeks before the election. We had no idea how heartbroken Brooklyn was about to be.

But the buildings were sold, and so we couldn't stay. Mike and I started looking at other spaces, and found one: a corner spot with a skylight and brick walls. A place that felt comfortable and warm. We wrote a business plan, and asked every bookseller we knew for advice. [We knew a lot of booksellers.]

The election happened, and what had seemed like two choices [open a bookstore, or move] now seemed like one [open a bookstore, the world is going to need solace and information]. Steve died, as if BookCourt's own center could not handle the transition. The store put up a sign in late December that they would be closing for good on New Year's Eve.

We signed the lease for Books Are Magic in February, and opened in May.

I loved BookCourt, but I don't think I ever grasped how much it meant to Henry and Mary and Zack and their family, how hard the work was, how endless. I knew about the margins, of course—that's the thing that people love to say to me now, when they know I own a bookstore. *Oof,* they say. *Must be tough.* It is. But what I didn't understand was the all-consuming nature of running a small business, and growing up in one. Just because I loved it, I thought it was mine.

There were some things I got right: There are generations of booksellers, in every store. Some of those waves are fantastic and some of those waves are tricky, but they always keep moving. Booksellers love candy and caffeine. There are always poets and intellectuals and eccentrics. Working for a family business sometimes means being told contradictory things. There are still movie stars—the same movie stars, and new ones. Everyone gets older, and most of the time, that means they are less guarded and more friendly. It is a privilege to be someone's bookseller, especially small children. It is a good idea to have giant bags of dog treats behind the counter. Books are meaningful things to provide.

But there are also things that I got wrong—mostly, that just because the store was open to the public, that the story belonged to me as much as it did to Henry and Mary. Mike and I have now owned Books Are Magic for four years, a tiny drop in the bucket of BookCourt's 35. Each year has been harder than the one before it. I email with Mary now and then, and I am always happy to tell her what I will tell the world now: *I don't know how you did it.* What I got wrong before was that just because I saw the place as an institution, because there were so many of us booksellers moving through the place, and so many thousands of books coming and going, and so many writers, that it was somehow impervious to pain, or struggle. I saw BookCourt the same way I saw the Natural History Museum, or the Met: as solid as a mountain face. Henry and Mary were private people—they remain so—and what it felt like to run a small business for three and a half decades was invisible to me. All I saw was the glamour of putting a book into someone's hand, and staying up late—BookCourt, you flirty scamp, you were open so *late*—talking and gossiping with friends when I should have been alphabetizing.

Before, I wished that BookCourt would last forever. Now I wish that someone, anyone, will love Books Are Magic as much as I loved BookCourt, that it will be a part of children's internal maps of their neighborhood, that couples will stroll the aisles together and flirt and marry, or flirt and not marry, but still think about those dates fondly. I hope that some of my booksellers will think of their time at the store as warmly as I think about BookCourt. I hope that my husband and I will get better and better at being bosses, which is a hard thing to learn.

Can you believe that bookstores exist? Heaven on earth—places full of books that you can bring home with you, to keep forever, or to give to someone you love. Do you know who has walked through our doors? Do you know the writers we've hosted? Have you ever watched a kid who has just learned how to read sit on the floor and just plow through a chapter book, one you know they'll finish before bed? Do you know how much I think about our booksellers, past and present, and how excited I am for the rest of their lives to unfold? Whatever BookCourt was, whatever Books Are Magic is, whatever your favorite bookstore was when you were a kid, or whatever your favorite bookstore is right now, that feeling is the same. It's huge, endless, infinite love. Come and see us sometime.

EMMA STRAUB is a New York City native, and is the author of the novels *All Adults Here*, *The Vacationers*, *Modern Lovers*, and *Laura Lamont's Life in Pictures*, as well as the short story collection *Other People We Married*. She and her husband own the independent bookstore Books Are Magic.

HERE COMES
THE NEIGHBORHOOD

Written by **MICHAEL DALY AND DENIS HAMILL**

Originally published by *The Village Voice* on July 25, 1977

The following Village Voice *cover story about the 1977 New York City blackout taps into complex issues of race, economic disparity and police brutality, equally relevant then and now in Brooklyn. In retrospect, that summer's crippling financial crisis, the Son of Sam murders and a scorching heat wave proved to be a terribly perfect storm. So, when the city lost power for two days that July, looting, vandalism, arson and hundreds of violent episodes [many involving law enforcement] became emblematic of a troubling era in the borough's history.*

The lights have been out for five minutes.

The people on Brooklyn's Broadway are going shopping.

Nineteen-year-old Jamar Jackson takes his second slug of pineapple soda as he watches his friend Bobby Stamps put his fist through the plate-glass window of Al-Bert's Men's Wear. Stamps reaches his bleeding hand past the shattered glass and grabs two shirts. An empty bottle of Wild Irish Rose crashes through another window. Now comes a brick. Hands are everywhere, stripping mannequins, grabbing shirts.

Jackson's heart is pounding. He snatches a pair of brown corduroy pants. He realizes how easy it is. A gun barks. Jamar runs onto the sidewalk and bumps into a man holding a .32 caliber automatic over his head. The man squeezes off five more shots. The muzzle flash lights up a gang of kids pulling on the grate covering the next store.

"They're hittin' Busches's Jewelry," somebody screams. More glass shatters. Jamar hears a stampede racing toward him in the darkness. Bodies press against him and carry him down the street.

Edwin Velez's television has been dead for 10 minutes. His girlfriend screams at him for not paying the Con Ed bill. Jumping off his tattered sofa, Edwin leans out his window. The entire neighborhood is dark. He hears glass breaking on Broadway, a half-block up Gates Avenue.

Edwin races into the hallway on the top floor of the four-story walk up. Neighbors are pushing and shouting in the stifling darkness.

"They're goin' in the stores," a woman yells. Edwin is knocked halfway down a flight of stairs by a sweat-soaked, 300-pound woman.

"Get out of my fuckin' way," the woman bellows as she tramples Edwin. "I'm goin' to get me something before the greedy niggers take it all." Edwin drags his 10-year-old cousin Cesar from the building's vestibule. On Gates Avenue, the stampede toward Broadway is on.

"Come on, man," Edwin tells Cesar. "It's a riot."

"That's when they come in and shoot you," Cesar says, pulling back into the vestibule.

"No, it's when you take what you want from the stores," Edwin says.

From the west, thousands pour out of a 630-acre slum called Bushwick. The area was first settled by the Dutch West India Company in 1660. The first blacks in Bushwick were slaves on the Dutch tobacco plantations. The Germans replaced the Dutch and were, in turn, squeezed out by the Irish. Then came the Poles and the Italians.

Today, there are no Dutch, Germans, Irish, Poles, or Italians. Today there are 225,000 blacks and Puerto Ricans living in 42,000 dwelling units. One quarter of these units have been classified by the City Planning Commission as "badly deteriorated." Bushwick High School, originally designed for an enrollment of 2000, has 3000 students. An average of 400 drop out each year.

From the east, thousands converge on Broadway from Bedford Stuyvesant.

Until 1940, Bed-Stuy was a middle-class enclave. But Harlem was bursting with immigrants from the South. Drawn by jobs at the Brooklyn Navy Yard and inspired by Duke Ellington's hit, "Take the A Train," an avalanche of poor blacks poured into Bed-Stuy via subway. After 25 years of blockbusting and redlining, Bed-Stuy was declared "the heart of the largest ghetto in America" by the Housing and Urban Development Administration.

On both sides of Broadway, unemployment hovers around 80 per cent. Half the families live on less than $4,000 a year. Forty per cent are on welfare. The infant mortality rate is the highest in the city. In 1967 the City Planning Commission reported that the area " ... urgently needs almost any type of community facility and service—housing, schools, health services, parks, supervised recreational activities, language classes, low-interest loans for home owners and businesses, social services, cultural activities, libraries, more job opportunities and learning programs, and improved sanitation and police protection. Assistance must be provided quickly."

> **"I'M GLAD THEY'RE DOING THIS," HARRY SAID, AS THE MOB CARTED OUT THE SHOE BOX'S INVENTORY.**

It is 10 years later, and the people on Broadway are assisting themselves.

Edwin and Cesar dash up to Broadway. Four men wrench a parking meter out of the concrete and batter the door of a jewelry store. On the third blow, the door blasts open. A crowd gathers. Edwin and Cesar are pushed into the store. A man with a baseball bat attacks the display cases. Broken glass sprays through the flashlight beams. A shard slices Edwin's cheek. Holding his shirttail to his face, Edwin feels around the dark floor. He finds two watch cases and slips them into his pocket.

The incoming tide of looters pushes Edwin and Cesar further into the store. It is pitch black and the heat is suffocating. Somebody has a transistor radio.

"There's a party atmosphere in Manhattan," a WINS newscaster says on the radio. Police sirens drown out the radio and probing beams of red light cut through the darkness. The tide turns and Edwin is carried toward the front of the store.

"God, don't shoot," a woman screams. Edwin steps on a leg as he scrambles for the exit. One cop beats a steady, sharp tattoo on the sidewalk with his riot stick. Three other cops simply watch the looters flee. On Gates Avenue, Edwin, breathing hard, opens the watch cases. They are empty.

"Shit, man," Edwin says. "All that for nothing. I was scared in there. My heart was doing a heavy tango."

Twelve-year-old Harry Brown stands outside the Everready Furniture Store. He is holding two notebooks he has just swiped from a stationery store. Across the street, a mob storms the Shoe Box. A year ago, Harry went into the Shoe Box to buy a pair of Pro-Keds. The shoes cost $12.82. Harry had $12.80.

"You don't get the shoes 'til you have the full amount," the white storekeeper had told Harry.

"I'm glad they're doing this," Harry said Wednesday night as the mob carted out the Shoe Box's inventory.

By now, Bobby Stamps has 200 pairs of dungarees, seven leather jackets, and dozens of shirts, all from Al-Bert's Men's Store. Nothing is left in the clothes store. Stamps races a stolen panel truck down Broadway from a luxury-item store called Time Credit.

A sign behind the accordion gates reads: COME IN. YOUR CREDIT IS GOOD WITH US. Bobby wraps a chain around the gates and hooks it to his truck's bumper. He pops the clutch and the truck jumps forward 30 feet. The accordion gates follow. Bobby heaves a garbage pail through the plate-glass window. Sixteen minutes later, he has five color television sets, two air conditioners, and a rack of wristwatches piled into his truck. Bobby stops to help an elderly man load a sofa onto the roof of a station wagon and races home.

"Plug them in and see if they work," Bobby's mother says as her son carts in the booty. Of course, there is no electricity.

Against all of this, Captain James Wynne of the 81st Precinct has only 22 men at his command. The station house's emergency generator kicks in moments after the lights go out. The first reports of looting come 10 minutes later. The dispatcher shouts that, along with the phones, the main radios are dead. The hand-sets will only receive.

Wynne orders the men in the station house into patrol cars and barks one simple command: "Stop the looters."

Wynne is in the lead car when the first cops hit Broadway. He and three other cops jump out in front of Time Credit. One last looter brushes past Wynne with a vacuum cleaner. The mob has moved up Broadway to another store. Wynne follows.

"We must have been outnumbered 70, maybe 80-to-1," a cop from the 81st Precinct says later. "And that was after reinforcements were brought in. I don't know how the hell nobody got killed. It must have been the magic of the blue."

The luxury items disappear into the tenements. Now, the shoe stores topple. Sneakers and high-heeled shoes litter the avenue. A young black kid races past two white cops with a paper bag full of shoes.

"Look, there goes a shoe-shine," one of the cops says. The other cop laughs. Youths swarm into the bike shops and ride away on the inventory. In the gloom, someone offers a $200 Peugeot 10-speed for $40. Duos zip from store to store on Mopeds, one kid driving, the other holding the swag.

A young black kid named Maurice Stone stands on the avenue with a new shirt, new jeans, and new sneakers.

"I wish I could get me some bikes," Stone says. "I been in a lot of stores, but I mostly got clothes. Most of the bikes is gone. I got a watch, but it don't work I don't think, so maybe I'm gonna sell it. "

The cops start to make the first collars. Two cops tackle a six-foot black man as he comes out of J. Michael's furniture store and drag him to a patrol car. Another cop grabs a teenager by her hair and pulls her toward the same car.

Two television sets, 11 pairs of Puma sneakers, and a sofa richer, 28-year-old Walter Bean ambles through the front window of the corner Key Food. Bean starts filling a shopping cart with meat.

"Fuck the whole thing," a tall man at the back of the store shouts. A match flares, but goes out. Another one sputters but also goes out.

"Anybody got any matches?" the tall man shouts. A middle-aged Puerto Rican woman stumbles back into the darkness. She hands matches to the tall man, but they drop to the floor. The tall man and Puerto Rican woman are now down on their knees searching for matches. The tall man finds them and kicks more papers into a pile he's already made against a back wall. The fire spreads and the smoke is soon rolling across the ceiling and curling up the side of the three-story building.

"Burn, baby, burn," the arsonist shouts, silhouetted against the orange glow of the flames. It isn't until the next day that anybody realizes 100 local part- and full-time jobs have also "burned, baby, burned."

Walter Bean escapes, pushing a shopping cart laden with chicken fryers, bacon, and ground chuck. The chicken fryers are marked at $1.08 a pound. The bacon is tagged at $1.60 a pound. The ground chuck is going for $1.49. At Sloan's on Sheridan Square in the West Village, the fryers go for 89 cents a pound, bacon for $1.35 a pound, and ground chuck for $1.39

a pound. Tonight, for the first time. Key Food is underselling Sloan's.

Fire trucks scream out of Engine Company's 222's station on Reid Street. By 4 a.m., there are fires raging on Broadway. There are not enough firemen to handle them. They head first for the buildings where people live. The El running above the avenue traps smoke and blocks the moonlight. The only light is from the shooting flames.

As the engines pour water into the blaze in Key Food, Dean Zule, 22, is in an alleyway on Green Street starting a barbecue. A neighbor brings down a can of lighter fluid and an armload of steaks. Zule turns the steaks with a screwdriver his brother stole from a hardware store. He raises his right hand, which is covered with a grimy, blood-stained bandage.

"The new sign is the fist with a towel wrapped around it," Zule says. "That's the power salute. This time it was flashlights, not guns. All power to the looters. Shit, I cut myself because I didn't have no towel."

Zule spits a steak with a screwdriver, gnaws on the suet, and breaks into a big, greasy grin. The sun is rising over Bushwick.

THURSDAY, JULY 14

Slats of sun lance through the tracks of the rusting El. Shards of plate glass glisten in the street. Debris is strewn along the sidewalks and gutters. Yawning policemen loiter on street corners, watching black children dressed in short pants and new sneakers scavenge in the litter. A dog with mange tears at a sooty steak in front of Key Food. A police helicopter cuts through the smoke that billows up from the burning buildings. Along a 34-block stretch, from Myrtle to Stone Street, store after store has been ripped open. Gates have been wrested from their runners. Cellar boards have been pried loose from their concrete foundations. Most of the saloons, liquor stores, fast-food joints, and storefront churches have not been touched.

Thousands of people are still in the streets. Music blares from new tape decks and transistor radios. Batteries are going for two dollars apiece. One man dances a soft shoe with a mannequin. More cops in riot gear troop onto the avenue. In small knots, people mutter that many of the cops are not wearing badges or nameplates. This, people say, is the first sign that the beatings and shootings are about to begin. One cop from the 83rd Precinct, badge number 15101, is asked why he wears no nameplate.

"Because we lost them," he answers. Another cop, standing in front of the Reid Avenue station house, brandishes a table leg as a weapon.

"I don't fucking feel like wearing no badge," he says. A heavyset cop, badge number 29065, races toward a dozen kids who are trying to match odd sneakers. His baton cracks a shin bone and the kids scatter. His nameplate is covered by a black elastic band.

Six kids sit on a rooftop, their legs dangling four stories above a team of firemen fighting a store blaze. A stream of water hits a 20-foot bed of embers. Dense smoke drives away the kids.

Twenty-seven fires are burning on Broadway. Great streams of water pour into the street from the fire sites, forming large black ponds at the blocked-up sewers. One exhausted fireman named Tommy O'Rourke stands shin-deep in a pond of water. A mannequin's arm floats next to O'Rourke's legs. He gulps from a glass of ice water. Black mucous runs from his nose. His teeth are creviced with soot. Sweat cuts through the black grime covering his face. His eyes are bloodshot. When he spits, his phlegm is black.

"It's a motherfucker," O'Rourke gasps. "When you're fighting a fire, been up all night, maybe 18 hours now, and you know the prick that lit this job is across the street laughing at you and probably torching another joint."

As the afternoon deepens, thousands more crowd onto the avenue. The power is back on. A J train thunders overhead. The looters cheer and then invade Vim's shoe store near Linden Boulevard. One woman sits on a burned-out car and measures her foot with a shoe-size ruler. A wedge of police move in on the store. Most of the looters flee. Some stay and exchange taunts with the police. Most of the cops edge away, their hands on their sidearms, their nervous eyes checking the rooftops for snipers. One cop rushes forward and clubs a Puerto Rican man with a bat. The other police pull the cop away from a fast-growing crowd.

"These motherfucking cops are pounding us," the Puerto Rican man says. "They ask no questions and they just beat your motherfucking head. They want static, motherfucker, they get static."

A black man with blood seeping from under his hair walks to the front door of the 81st Precinct.

"I want to talk to your boss," the man tells a cop stationed at the door. "One of your boys hit me upside my head just because I was carrying a pipe."

"What were you carrying a pipe for?" the cop asks.

"Shit man," the complainant says. "Just 'cause you carry a pipe doesn't mean you're gonna use it."

Then the power dies again. The stop lights are out. Tires screech. Horns blare. Police sirens wail. Shouting matches break out. The sound of breaking glass picks up.

A squad of Savage Skulls appears, flying their war colors, carrying longer sticks than the cops.

"God is giving the poor people their bread today," a gang member named Smokey says. "The poor people only want the same things the cops have. TVs, nice furniture, shit like that. And food. People have to eat. The cops are lucky they don't want blood. But before this is over there might be some blood anyway."

> **"I'M SCARED. IT'S THE APOCALYPSE OUT THERE. IF THIS GETS WORSE, I'M MOVING BACK TO BARBADOS."**

"The cops started this shit, man." Blue Eyes, the supreme president of the 14th Regiment of the Bushwick Division of the Savage Skulls, says. "They're taking things off looters, my people, and putting it in their cars and takin' it home to their houses, man. One cop broke a little girl's hip. The cops are handling it all wrong, They beating up black and Puerto Rican people. The cops should be in the stores. If there was a cop in a store, nobody is gonna go in there and risk getting killed for a pair of sneakers." Blue Eyes points across the street. Two cops in riot gear are guarding a burned-out Key Food. A hundred yards down the street, people are leaving a grocery store with six-packs of warm beer.

"I went to some of the precincts," Blue Eyes says. "I told some of the brass there that they doin' it wrong. I know some of the brass. I been on TV shows with 'em. You know what they told me? They told me to kiss their ass. Well, if that's what they want, we'll handle this shit. We had 82 guys here this morning. I'm thinkin' of calling in all the gangs and handling this thing right. We have a right to protect our community against police brutality and shit. We might finish this thing off completely, man, tonight."

And now, the night is here and there are no lights. Bands of youths rove the avenue toting two-foot flashlights, baseball bats, iron pipes, two-by-fours, and even hammers. The police wander aimlessly up and down the street. Every 20 minutes a caravan of eight patrol cars crawls down Broadway. The looting pauses as the cars pass, then continues. People talk in low tones. There is too much tension to shout.

Seventy-five looters have been arrested and packed into the pens at the Reid Street station. In the booking room, stolen goods are piled head high.

"What do they expect us to do with all this shit?" one cop asks another.

"Who the fuck cares?" the other answers. "We'll just shovel it into barrels and send it down to the Property Clerk's office. Let them figure it out. The entire garage outside is already filled. This is just the overflow."

A third cop is in the rear of the precinct taking inventory. After 24 hours on the street, he was ordered back to the station, and handed a clipboard and a stack of forms.

"Where the fuck is that other Quasar TV?" he says to another cop.

"How the fuck should I know?" the second cop says. "I only dealt with Zeniths."

"I feel like a fucking stock boy," says the first.

"A stock boy with a gun," says the second.

"Fuck you," says the cop with clipboard. "Now where is that other Quasar?" He is asked how many television sets were brought in. He answers, turning into a salesman. "You interested in a floor model or a portable?" Turning back into a cop, he says, "I honestly don't know. I have one here, a Quasar, I can't even find. It might be buried under that mountain of shit."

He points to the mountain of shit. It includes: paper towels, frozen pizzas, baby clothes, Kotex, Pampers, jackets, lounge chairs, mattresses, couches, lawn mowers, vacuum cleaners, dishes, silverware, and hundreds of other items.

A detective walks up to the cop.

"I heard you need a hand," the detective says, offering the cop a mannequin's hand.

Over at the desk, a sergeant points to a porcelain statue of Stan Laurel.

"Can you imagine going to jail for stealing that?" the sergeant asks. "This is another fine mess Stan Laurel has gotten somebody into."

At the other end of the room, a half-dozen civilians huddle on plastic chairs. They've come to the precinct for safety.

"I'm spending the night right here," one of the civilians, Teddy Eve says. "I'm scared. It's the apocalypse out there. If this gets worse, I'm moving back to Barbados. There's no money in Barbados, but they don't have no apocalypse down there."

"I was terrified something would happen to me," a West Indian woman sitting on the next chair says. "It's horrible, just horrible. It's all been destroyed." A minister from Bed-Stuy stands in the doorway. Earlier in the day, Mayor Beame had put out a call for all religious leaders to cruise their neighborhoods to "restore the calm."

"I went out there," the minister says. "But they all too busy stealin'."

The power comes on at 9:30. Thirty-seven officers sit in the muster room, waiting for the next caravan run. Black cops stay in tight knots. They only join white cops at 9:50, when it's time for another sweep. Donning helmets and swinging sticks, the cops jump into the row of squad cars.

By the time the cops hit Broadway, the crowds have moved away from the avenue's streetlights and dispersed into the dark side streets.

"There's nothing left to steal that's worth getting shot over," a middle-aged black man says as he walks down Putnam Street. "And I know that if this goes on much longer, the cops will be shooting."

Arson is now the main event. On the corner of Somers and Stone Avenue, a five-story warehouse is blazing out of control. The first alarm had come in at 5:30 p.m. By 6 it had reached five alarms. It is now 10:30 and the blaze is still out of control. A super-pumper has been brought in. Crowds from Broadway move in to watch the show. Seven firemen have already been injured.

The fire jumps 50 feet across the street. Three other buildings and two cars catch fire. The factory's cornice crumbles, crushing a fire chief's van.

Miguel Perez, 20, who lives in the last remaining house on the block, watches the blaze. He claims he saw a man light the fire.

"This cop hit a tall, skinny, colored guy when he caught him looting the warehouse," Perez says. "There was stereos, TVs, clothes—that kind of stuff. So this guy gets mad because the cop hit him. He comes back later with two red gasoline cans and pours them into the building. He lit that gas up. Then he soaked some of the other buildings in gasoline." Part of the factory collapses, sending columns of sparks 100 feet into the night sky.

"I gotta make sure this guy don't torch my place, man," Perez continues. "I'm telling you, I know this guy's face. I've seen him in the neighborhood. Me and my two brothers are gonna fuck this guy up good. Maybe I'll kill him. I haven't decided yet. He had a big wide Afro. I'd like to burn it off."

Tonight is the night of the fire union election. Michael Maye has lost to Richard Vizzini. Neither of them has come out to Bushwick. So far, neither has Beame or Fire Commissioner O'Hagan. Deputy Chief Tortoriello has—since the lights went out.

"Nah, they ain't been out here," Tortoriello says. "That's the big time. This is only Brooklyn." He chuckles and returns to the fire.

FRIDAY, JULY 15

The fire burns through the night. At daybreak Michael Perez is still standing watch. He says he will not go to sleep until he is sure the arson and rampage are finished. As the warehouse continues to smolder, people start to reappear on Broadway.

"It looks like Sherman marched through here on his way to Atlanta," says one morning stroller.

Those stores that were not hit are opening for business. Paul Alexander, the manager of National Shoes near Linden Boulevard explains that, although his store went untouched, business is bad.

"There has been no business today," he says. "There won't be for a long time. Everybody around here has new shoes."

Up the street, Eddy Mizihi sits in a cream-colored Plymouth outside of what was once his clothing store.

"I might open it again," Mizihi says, "If Mayor Beame gives me the money. If not ... what am I going to do?"

Ahmed Muharran stands in front of his grocery at 1385 Broadway. He hasn't slept in 48 hours. From the moment of the blackout until this morning, he stood in the doorway to his shop with a double-barreled shotgun. Right now he's open for business, but he keeps a police baton in his hand.

"Look, you have to protect yourself," Ahmed says, keeping his eye on a 12-year-old standing near the potato-chip rack. "I told them when they tried coming in they were going to get hurt. They went away and robbed somebody else. Maybe tonight I'll sleep. We'll see."

Outside Ahmed's store, Rodney Washington and Wallace H. Jones are discussing the situation.

"This Con Edison makes me laugh," Washington says. "They blaming the whole goddamned thing on some act of God. Now how can they say that when Con Edison is God?"

"I don't give a damn who's to blame," says Jones. "What I want to know is where the fuck was the Civil Defense? The Civil Defense is supposed to help the police. I know because me, Wallace H. Jones of 710 Bushwick Avenue, was in the Civil Defense for 11 years. The Civil Defense is supposed to be here when the bomb drop. *Well the bomb done dropped.*"

Jones, who became a building contractor after he retired from the Civil Defense, walks into Al-Bert's Men's Wear next door to Ahmed's grocery store.

"You need some repair work in here?" Jones asks Maurice Phillips, the owner of Al-Bert's. Phillips looks around the store. The windows are smashed. The bare shelves are splintered.

"Maybe," says Phillips, laughing. Phillips first came into the store 11 years ago to buy a pair of pants on a layaway plan. A salesman told Phillips that the store needed a stock boy. For the next four years, Phillips stacked shirts and pants for $95 a week, an exceptional wage for black workers on Broadway. In 1970, Phillips took out a Small Business Administration loan and bought out the white owners of the shop. Phillips started to experience what he calls the "pitfalls for black businessmen." Factories sent him inferior merchandise and refused to give refunds on damaged clothing. In 1974, Phillips grossed $274,000, but not a single bank would extend him a loan. Two years ago, the store's basement flooded, destroying $70,000 worth of clothing. According to Phillips, the landlord, Broadway Realty, Inc., refused to accept responsibility for the damage and shortly thereafter, raised the rent. Phillips was hit by a spate of break-ins and hired the Holmes Protection Agency to watch his store. For $387 a month, Holmes promised to call Phillips the moment the burglar alarm went off. Last year, Holmes twice let the alarm ring for more than nine hours. Phillips was cleaned out both times. At the same time, the Chemical Bank was sitting on a $15,000 installment of Phillips's second $60,000 SBA loan.

"You're a turkey," an officer at Chemical recently told Phillips. "You're headed for bankruptcy. We've been telling you that for a year."

"Then why aren't I bankrupt?" Phillips asked. "You refuse to give me any working capital and I'm still in business."

"I was looted before the riot," Phillips says. "The people were looted, too. You have to look at the total economic condition, the frame of mind of the people. I'm more angry at Chemical Bank than I am at the people. Window shopper finally got a chance to fulfill their desires and not just live with the bare necessities. Everybody stepped into the television commercials for a few hours and took what they wanted."

As Phillips talks, the mayor and an entourage drive past the store in two air-conditioned buses. When the buses stop farther up the block, the mayor and 50 reporters and cameramen exit onto Broadway. Fire engines are parked at crazy angles along the streets. Smoke still wafts from some of the ruins. A hydrant is still gushing on the corner. The stream of water runs swiftly along the curb, carrying assorted debris—cancelled checks, price tags, pages from ledgers, mail orders, the scribbled paperwork of small businesses. Beame, with the help of an aide, hops over the stream and starts talking to newsmen.

"Jobs, jobs, jobs, how about some jobs," a group of black kids on the other side of the street chant.

"He's here to discuss foreign aid," one reporter jokes. Exactly 11,360 feet of news film is shot of the mayor as he walks through the devastation. The mayor directs an aide to expedite emergency housing to a woman burned out of her apartment. The woman kisses the mayor's hand.

"What's all this?" a black youth asks a friend.

"They making a commercial," the friend answers.

Mayoral candidate Bella Abzug is also in the area. At the 81st Precinct, she examines the loot piled in the building's garage. Dressed in a sporty summer dress, Abzug says she still stands behind the right of policemen and firemen to strike.

"What if they went on strike during something like this?" she is asked.

"They wouldn't," she answers.

"What would you do if you were the mayor?"

"Mobilize the community organizations and get them into the streets."

After Abzug leaves, Gary Jenkins, a local resident says: "The community was mobilized. They were all out lootin'." Jenkins grabs a shopping cart and pushes it down the street.

"Going shopping?" Jenkins is asked.

"No," Jenkins says, "I already been."

Ron Shiffman, director of the Pratt Institute's urban planning center, is also in the neighborhood.

"This whole thing about giving out Small Business Administration loans to merchants who lost their businesses is a sham," Shiffman says. "There isn't the structure for giving out the loans. The mayor is playing politics with people's lives. It's an ugly thing to see all this looting, for sure. But the people who live in Bed-Stuy and Bushwick have had their lives looted for years."

Shiffman comes from the Bud-Stuy tradition inspired by Robert Kennedy in the early 1960s. Speaking at a community meeting in Bed-Stuy in 1966, Kennedy talked about the future that arrived on Wednesday:

"If this community can become an avenue of opportunity then others will take heart ... but if this community fails, then others will falter and the noble dream of equality and dignity will fall with it."

As night falls on Broadway, only the people who live here every day remain.

Bobby Stamps is hawking $36 French-cut jeans on a street corner for $8 a pair. Jamar Jackson is with him, wearing a gold Aries necklace. Jackson is an Aquarius.

"I wish there would be a blackout every night," Stamps says. "Shit, I'd be a millionaire."

On the roofs of the Bushwick housing projects off Fulton Street, a huge clearance sale is under way. Hundreds of tenants examine piles of televisions, stereos, appliances, and shotguns. A 15-year-old is handing out complimentary cassettes with each tape recorder. Most of the merchandise is going for less than 10 per cent of retail value.

Along the avenue, the bars are doing their usual business. Music and drunks float out of Beulah's Goodtimers, the Utopia Lounge, and Jukes Lounge. A transit cop is ticketing a battered Chevy parked at a bus stop. Groups of Puerto Ricans sit around card tables on milk boxes and play dominoes. Salsa blares from a new tape deck. The stores along Broadway are either shuttered or gutted. There is already graffiti on some of the plywood covering the broken windows. In yellow spray paint, someone has written: DETROIT.

Blue Eyes and Smokey of the Savage Skulls stroll down the street.

"I'm glad it cooled out last night," Blue Eyes says. "The police kept cool and it worked out. It's better that way. Maybe the cops will try to understand the street people."

Inside the 81st Precinct, Captain Wynne is ready to go home. He looks exhausted, but agrees to answer some questions.

"Did you expect the looting?" he is asked.

"You expect what you get," Wynne says. "But I'm not surprised."

"Do you expect any more trouble?"

"Not if we keep the lights on."

"Why weren't the cops wearing badges and nameplates?"

"I wasn't looking at cops."

"Have there been any arrests for violent crimes in the past three days?"

"No."

Behind Wynne, there is a bulletin board with a dozen pictures pinned to it. WANTED FOR MURDER, a sign above the picture reads. Last year, there were 23 murders, 50 reported rapes, and 1100 armed robberies in the 81st Precinct.

"It was a bitch," a desk sergeant says after Wynne leaves. "But at least nobody got hurt bad. You'll see the violence start up again, though. Now that the party's over, it'll get back to the nitty gritty. We'll have a stiff by morning." The sergeant goes back to his bacon, lettuce, and tomato sandwich.

DENIS HAMILL is a former columnist for the New York *Daily News* and current staff writer and executive story editor for *Law & Order: SVU*. He won the prestigious Meyer Berger Award for best New York City reporting. He has written for *New York Magazine*, the *Los Angeles Herald Examiner* and *New York Newsday*.

MICHAEL DALY is a correspondent with *Newsweek* and *The Daily Beast*. He was previously a columnist with the *New York Daily News* and a staff writer with *New York Magazine*. He was a finalist for the Pulitzer Prize for commentary in 2002 for his columns on 9/11.

INDEX

INDEX

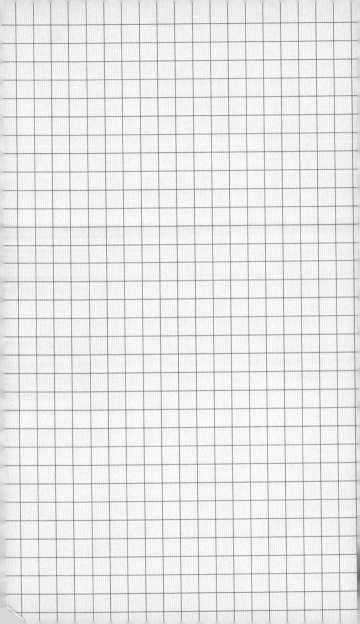

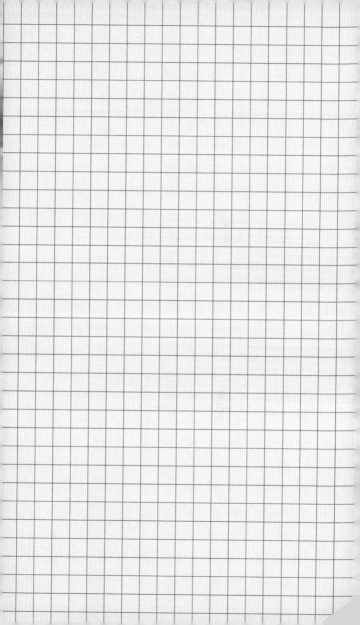

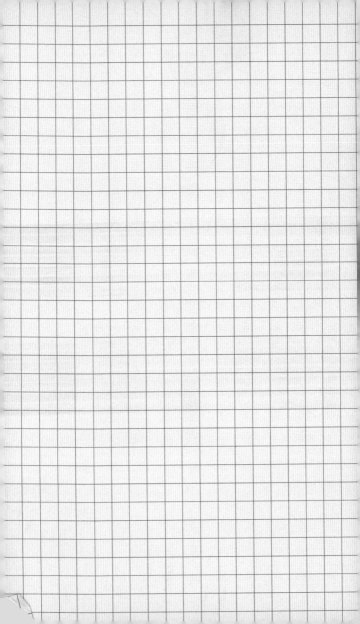